*Is Your
Retirement
at Risk?*

Is Your Retirement at Risk?

Winning Strategies for a Financially Secure Future

Ranga Chand
and Sylvia Carmichael

Published in 2002 by
Stoddart Publishing Co. Limited
895 Don Mills Road, 400-2 Park Centre
Toronto, Canada M3C 1W3

www.stoddartpub.com

To order Stoddart books please contact General Distribution Services
Tel. (416) 213-1919   Fax (416) 213-1917
Email cservice@genpub.com

10   9   8   7   6   5   4   3   2   1

National Library of Canada Cataloguing in Publication Data

Chand, Ranga
Is your retirement at risk?: winning strategies for a financially secure future

ISBN 0-7737-6281-7

1. Retirement income — Canada — Planning.   2. Financial security.
I. Carmichael, Sylvia D.   II. Title.

HG179.C385   2002   332.024'01   C2002-900735-6

This book contains information and statistics that have been obtained from
sources that are believed to be reliable but cannot be guaranteed as to accuracy
or completeness. This book is for information only and should not be construed
as investment advice or a recommendation to buy, sell, or hold any securities.
It is strongly recommended that readers seek advice from legal, financial,
or accounting professionals before making any investment decisions.

Cover Design: Bill Douglas at the Bang

Text design and typesetting: Kinetics Design & Illustration

THE CANADA COUNCIL | LE CONSEIL DES ARTS
FOR THE ARTS | DU CANADA
SINCE 1957 | DEPUIS 1957

*We acknowledge for their financial support of our publishing program the Canada Council,
the Ontario Arts Council, and the Government of Canada through the
Book Publishing Industry Development Program (BPIDP).*

Printed and bound in Canada

To Jason

Contents

3 Sources of Retirement Income

4 Funding Your Retirement

5 **Living Longer and Living Better:
The Keys to a Financially Secure Retirement**

Acknowledgements

We would like to express our thanks to Nelson Doucet and Donald G. Bastian of Stoddart Publishing for their advice, enthusiasm, and unfailing support in the preparation of *Is Your Retirement at Risk?* We are also very grateful to our editor, Gillian Watts, whose editing talents are in great evidence throughout the book. A special thank-you also to Sue Sumeraj for proofreading and to Daniel Crack for the book's design and typesetting.

Introduction

At some point in the future you are going to retire. Whether you do so willingly or reluctantly, it will still happen. With no regular salary cheque to rely on, you will have to depend on government programs, company pensions, and your own savings to provide you with an adequate retirement income.

Savings patterns show that many Canadians will not have enough money to maintain their pre-retirement standard of living when they stop working. What's more, many middle-to-high-income families may not be able to replace even two-thirds of their earnings. This means that on retirement, their standard of living will drop by over 30%! If government programs become less generous in the future, which many experts believe will be the case, the drop will be even more precipitous. What's more, extended lifespans, coupled with a landscape in which one out of every four Canadians is a senior, may mean that sometime in the future, government programs could start at a later age, at 67 or possibly even later.

In order to provide for a secure retirement, you need to take control of your financial future. This book provides a comprehensive, easy-to-understand, and practical blueprint for achieving a financially secure retirement. It also explains how changes to Canada's health care system and public pensions will affect retirees.

The book's aim is to help readers

- determine, using the worksheet in the appendices, how much they will need to retire comfortably
- find out which government programs they are eligible for and how much they will get
- estimate the worth of their company pension plan
- calculate if they have a retirement income gap and how to bridge that gap
- ensure a sustainable retirement income for an extended lifespan
- grasp the effects of bull and bear markets on retirement incomes
- come to terms with safe withdrawal rates
- deal with fluctuating income streams
- find out how to set up a worry-free strategic retirement portfolio
- prosper from the coming boom in longevity-related industries

Extended lifespans — which could mean retirements of 30+ years — will give many Canadians the opportunity to embark on second-life careers. It will allow others to dust off and pursue personal dreams and aspirations. But neither of these options will be available if your retirement income is inadequate. Take the time *now* to ensure that you are one of the fortunate ones.

1

The New Realities of Retirement

The Changing Face
of Retirement

Retirement as an accepted and, indeed, expected phase of life is a relatively new phenomenon. At the turn of the 20th century, most workers in the developed nations of the world worked until they died, which was often early. Those who made it into their early 70s and were no longer able to work spent only a few brief years in retirement, being looked after by their children. The more children they had, the higher the likelihood that somebody would be there to care for them. If the extended family didn't help out, the old had to rely on charity — the forerunner of today's pensions — which was organized mainly by religious groups. In many cases, to be old and unable to work was to be destitute.

A Brief History of Retirement Pensions

Pensions in some form or another have been around since the time of ancient Rome, when benefits were paid to disabled or elderly soldiers who had served the Republic. In North America, starting with the American Revolution in 1775, the United States also rewarded its war veterans with retirement benefits. Public servants in France and Britain in the early 1800s were the next group to enjoy an established pension system. This was followed by the first general social security program, which was introduced in Germany in the 1880s, under the direction of Chancellor Otto von Bismarck.

Bismarck's program was not altogether an act of altruism on his part, but more of a political ploy to gain support from the German workers for his own party and derail his opponents — which goes to show that things haven't changed that much. What's more, when Bismarck introduced the program, the retirement age was set at 65, at a time when very few workers lived long enough to collect the pension.

Despite those early initiatives, it was only in the past century that income security programs for the elderly as a group were securely established. With the advent of the Industrial Revolution, young people began leaving the farms and the surrounding coun-tryside for opportunities in the big cities, leaving their elderly parents and grandparents to fend for themselves. At that point gov-ernment stepped in, and state-supported social welfare programs grew rapidly. By the 1930s, most of the world's industrialized nations had some type of public welfare program.

The United States did not have a universal social security pro-gram until 1935. Triggered by the Great Depression, the Social Security Act was passed as part of President Franklin D. Roosevelt's "New Deal" program. When the program was initiated, social secu-rity benefits to retirees were payable in the form of a single lump sum. One of the earliest beneficiaries of the lump-sum benefit was an appli-cant who retired one day after the program began. For a nickel's worth of contributions, the retiree received a one-time payment of 17 cents. Monthly benefit payments began in 1940; the first monthly retirement cheque — in the amount of $22.54 — was paid out in January of that year to a retired legal secretary. During her 35 years of collecting her monthly cheque, she received over $22,000 in benefits.

In Canada, the first income security program for the elderly was introduced in 1927, providing recipients with the grand sum of $240 a year. Fortunately, Old Age Security (OAS), which was estab-lished in 1952, currently provides a bit more to pensioners, with annual benefits of around $5,000. Moreover, the Canada Pension Plan and the Quebec Pension Plan were set up in 1966 to provide increased income security for workers and their families. The poverty rate of the elderly in Canada, as with other developed countries, is now comparable to that of the remainder of the population. This dramatic change from a hundred years before can be attributed in large part to the creation of these social programs.

Today, however, the long-term viability of most social security programs is under intense scrutiny and is being hotly debated, mainly because of the unprecedented structural shift in the population now underway. In all of human history, the elderly (those age 65 and over) have never accounted for more than 2% to 3% of the total population. Now, the elderly in all industrial countries account for almost 12.5%, and by the year 2050 this proportion is projected to rise to 25%. In other words, one of every four people will be over 65 years old. What's more, the elderly are going to be around for what could be a very long time.

The Longevity Factor

In Canada at the beginning of the 19th century, life expectancy at birth was a meagre 35 years. Today the average life expectancy for Canadians who reach 65 years of age is about 82 years for men and 85 years for women. But if you take a look at a typical life expectancy table, you will find that the vast majority of men will die between 74 and 94 years of age, while women tend to die between 77 and 96 years old.

Canadians who are 85 and older — the "old old" — are the fastest growing age group within our society; they will increase in numbers from about 445,000 in 2001 to just over 930,000 by 2026. This opens up the very real possibility that many more Canadians will live to become centenarians.

In 2001 the number of centenarians in Canada stood at about 4,300. By 2046, the year the first baby boomers hit 100, that number will climb to over 45,000. Being a woman helps. Today there are about 3,600 female centenarians and only 700 or so men. A woman of 65 who has no history of heart disease or cancer in her family, is a non-smoker, and has a healthy, active lifestyle can quite reasonably expect to live to be close to 100.

In the United States, the number of Americans 85 and older will also rise. According to a CSIS National Commission on Retirement Policy fact sheet, while the 65-and-over population will double by 2050, the 85-and-over group will triple or even quadruple by 2040. As in Canada, the number of elderly living to 100 will also increase dramatically.

On a global scale, according to the United Nations report *The State of the World Population 1998*, the number of people surviving to 100 will grow to 2.2 million by 2050, 16 times more than in 1998. Moreover, this segment of society will be the fastest-growing population group (a statistic not lost on the greeting card business, which now offers at least ten different ways to say "happy 100th").

Although improved health care, medical advances, and higher standards of living have played a large part in extending lifespan, scientists are also in hot pursuit of the gene or genes that may determine just how long we can live. While this may seem a bit like hunting for a needle in a haystack — make that 1,000+ haystacks — substantial progress has already been made. In the summer of 2001, scientists at Harvard University and two Boston-area hospitals reported in the *Proceedings of the National Academy of Sciences* that they have already isolated the chromosome segment that decides heredity. The bigger task may be locating the gene or genes that determine longevity.

Yet with these increases in lifespan, there are potential downsides. People who live longer will also have to draw a retirement income for longer. To put it another way, they will have to save more now or learn to live on less later. As many baby boomers have high levels of personal debt, low savings, and uncertain company pensions, their future retirement lifestyles look anything but promising.

Another fly in the proverbial ointment is the possibility that the "normal" retirement age, which is currently 65, may be adjusted upwards. This has already been set in motion in the United States, where the retirement age for full social security benefits will gradually increase to the age of 67 by 2022. If the human lifespan keeps getting longer — and given continued medical advances, there is no reason it shouldn't — one can reasonably expect that at some point in the future the normal retirement age will be pegged to life expectancy. And on reflection, we may indeed determine as a society that the right age to retire is not necessarily 65.

Of course, when it comes to life expectancies, we still have some way to go to catch up with a few other species. Some varieties of tortoise, for instance, live an average of 150 years, and herpetologists estimate that alligator snapping turtles can live to at least 300 years, and maybe even to 500. Although they probably have their own problems to worry about, pensions won't be one of them.

Baby Boomers and the New Retirement Paradigm

The first wave of baby boomers, those born between 1946 and 1964, will start retiring at age 60 in about 2005, and at age 65 in 2010. Many of these boomers look at their parents' generation as a yardstick of what to expect in retirement. However, what they see may not be what they get. The previous generation benefited from expanded public pensions, job security, double-digit inflation in the 1970s and 1980s that wiped out their mortgages, and tremendous increases in real incomes. The baby boomers have not been so fortunate. The idyllic scenario of wintering in warmer climates and enjoying a generous retirement income may be only a fading dream for many of them. Instead, the future could be decidedly chilly.

Back in the 1960s there were about eight workers paying into the Canada Pension Plan for every senior collecting benefits. With those kinds of numbers, the CPP was as solid as a rock, and no pensioner wasted a nanosecond worrying about whether or not the next benefit cheque was in the mail.

Unfortunately for tomorrow's retirees, the post-war baby boom was followed by a baby bust — women were choosing careers over motherhood in record numbers. By 2030, when the first wave of boomers are in their 80s and feeling vulnerable, the number of workers paying into the Canada Pension Plan will have dropped dramatically to three for every one senior. Even though rigorous steps have been taken to secure the long-term viability of the program, there is still a sense that the ground beneath our feet isn't quite as solid as it used to be. And if you are looking at your company pension plan to take up the slack, you may need to look elsewhere.

These days, companies are moving away from the old-style defined benefit pension that guaranteed employees a retirement income for life, the kind your parents probably enjoy. You put in your 30 or more years with the company, and at the end of your career you received a cheque for a fixed dollar amount every month for the rest of your life — nice and straightforward and secure. Today, although they are still offering employees the benefits of a pension plan, many companies are switching to defined contribution plans. While these more flexible plans are suitable for today's more mobile workforce and have the potential to provide more in retirement than a defined benefit plan, they place the onus of providing a retirement income securely on the employee's shoulders. The final outcome is a lot less certain. (For more on these types of pension plans, see Chapter 9.)

Canadians are also not saving nearly as much as they used to. The personal savings rate, which reached a high of 20.1% in 1982, plummeted to 3.9% in 2000. We have become a nation of rampant consumers. According to Statistics Canada, the average Canadian family carries approximately $14,000 on a line of credit, $3,000 on credit cards, $11,000 in vehicle loans, and $9,300 in "other debts." That's a whopping $37,300, not including mortgages. In 2000, Canadian household debt — including mortgages — reached an unprecedented 97.4% of disposable income. What's more, according to Industry Canada, as of the end of October 2000 we had almost $34 billion in outstanding balances on our credit cards. While Canadians are racking up the purchases, the banks are doing very nicely, taking in around $6 billion in interest payments alone, every year.

By the beginning of the 21st century, many boomers owned, or nearly owned, their own homes. However, home ownership may not turn out to be the safety net they had counted on. It is doubtful that the hot real estate market of the past, which through sheer numbers the boomers helped orchestrate, will be repeated. Also, the double-digit inflation of the 1970s and 1980s that helped fuel real estate prices has not re-emerged; consequently, the prospects for high capital gains are dim.

Add to all of this the new reality of our extended lifespan, and the retirement picture for baby boomers gets less and less bright. The rallying cry of "freedom 55" that resounded across the retirement landscape in the latter part of the 20th century may soon be replaced with "freedom 65." And even that could be overly optimistic.

The Greying of Canada

Imagine a Canada where the coffee shops are not only frequented by the old, but staffed by them as well. Where the target group for advertising is not the 18-to-45-year-olds, but those who are 65 and over. And where walkers, not baby strollers and in-line skates, dominate the sidewalks. Not in my lifetime, you say? Think again. This is a brief glimpse of what life will be like in Canada by the year 2050. Welcome to your future.

The total population of Canada is projected to increase over the next 50 years from 31 million in 2000 to over 41 million by 2050. But it's the population mix that will undergo the most dramatic change. The number of seniors in Canada — those age 65 and over — ballooned from just over a million in the middle of the 20th century to about 4 million at the beginning of the 21st century. By the time we reach the middle of this century, it is projected that there will be over 10 million elderly Canadians.

At the same time, the working-age population — those between 20 and 64 — is expected to increase by only 3.5 million, rising to 22.7 million by 2050. Furthermore, the youth population — those age 20 and under — is expected to increase by a mere 300,000 over the next 50 years. By 2050, young people will number about 8.4

million and account for only 20% of the population, down from 26% at the turn of this century.

Of course, this major structural shift is not all caused by increased lifespan. The "birth dearth" that followed the baby boom from 1967 to 1979 has also played its part. Still, although fertility trends may move up or down in the future, an extended lifespan is here to stay.

Canada Is Not Alone

By 2050, when the total world population hits the 9-billion mark, the proportion of seniors is expected to rise to over 16%, or around 1.4 billion. According to the United Nations Population Division's latest report, *World Population Prospects: The 2000 Revision*, the global increase in the number of "old old" — those 80 years and over — will be particularly striking. This segment of the world population is expected to increase more than fivefold, rising from 69 million in 2000 to a staggering 379 million in 2050.

In a number of the industrialized nations, including Germany, Italy, and Japan, the size of the senior population has already surpassed that of the child population (those age 14 and under). By 2050 there will be more seniors than children in every major industrial country. According to the U.S. Census Bureau, the number of seniors in the major industrialized countries of the world is expected to almost double to close to 200 million by the year 2050. The steepest increases will occur in North America, with the fastest growth expected right here in Canada. Table 1a demonstrates the projected growth of the senior population over the next 50 years.

The Economic Implications of an Aging Society

Over the next 50 years, all the industrial nations of the world will have to deal with the consequences of low fertility rates and increased life expectancies. In order to gauge the effect of these demographic changes, policy-makers will be paying close attention to the depend-

Table 1a

Growth of the Senior (65+) Population in Major Industrial Countries

	2000	2050	% change
Canada	3.9 (millions)	10.3 (millions)	+164%
United States	34.7	82.0	+136%
France	9.5	16.0	+68%
Germany	13.4	22.8	+70%
Italy	10.4	16.2	+56%
United Kingdom	9.3	15.7	+69%
Japan	21.6	34.3	+59%
Total	**102.8**	**197.3**	**+92%**

Source: U.S. Census Bureau

ency ratio, the number of people of working age (20–64) compared to those 65 years of age and over.

At the beginning of the 21st century, out of a total population of about 700 million in the G7 countries, around 420 million, or 60%, were of working age. By 2050 the total working-age population in these countries is expected to shrink by between 5 and 10 million, while the dependent elder population, those age 65 and over, will expand by close to 100 million. Thus, by the middle of this century, each person age 65 or over will be supported by just over two people of working age, as compared with about four today.

Most analysts contend that an aging population will have a detrimental impact on a country's economic growth and standards of living through its impact on three factors: supply of labour, aggregate savings, and technological innovation.

As the rate of growth of the labour force slows down, the burden on the smaller group of workers to support an aging population will increase. This increased burden could lead to higher taxes on the working population, which may in turn dent the work effort and further retard needed increases in the supply of labour. Clearly, under such a scenario, economic growth would likely suffer and further strain a nation's ability to meet its fiscal obligations.

The number crunchers also anticipate a decline in public savings and a concomitant rise in government budget deficits. This projected decrease in savings is based on the anticipated increase in age-related public expenditures, of which pensions are at the top of the list for most countries. In a recent study by the Paris-based Organisation for Economic Cooperation and Development (OECD) on the fiscal implications of aging, age-related spending on public pensions in Canada is expected to jump from 5% of the nation's output to 11% by 2050. Similarly, health care spending is projected to account for a significantly larger portion of the nation's output over the next 50 years, rising from about 6% of the GDP in 2000 to 10.5% by 2050. Moreover, cross-country projections conclude that the generosity of our public pension systems in general is on a downward trend.

When it comes to the effect of an aging society on productivity and technological progress, the prognosis is mixed. One camp strongly asserts that an aging work force will be slower and consequently less productive. They argue that a less productive labour force will, over time, lead to a slower rate of growth in standards of living. But counter-theory holds that a labour shortage could actually push technological innovation to new levels, thereby enhancing productivity and offsetting the decrease in the workforce. Under such a scenario, the effect of an aging society on standards of living would be minimal.

Of course, all of these projections and predictions are based on various assumptions about demographic trends and other economic variables. But the underlying message is clear: Unless the negative growth effect of aging can be offset by a combination of higher labour force participation rates and increased productivity growth, governments will have to deal with a shrinking tax base in the future. This in turn will result in serious budgetary restraints, the impact of which could be felt most significantly in universal programs for the elderly, such as pensions and health care.

Soft Landings

Naturally, with any set of problems there are also potential solutions. Answers to a shrinking workforce could lie in such key initiatives as raising the normal age of retirement, providing incentives to increase the workforce participation rate of both women and men (particularly in the 55-to-64 age group), and increased immigration. Besides having extended lifespans, people are living healthily for longer, so many workers might not be averse to staying on the job for a few more years. A great number of them might even welcome such an outcome, which would give them a chance not only to accumulate more savings for retirement, but also to remain a productive part of society for longer.

Monetary and other incentives, such as expanded daycare facilities, could attract and keep more women in the workforce. And birth rates in some countries may trend upwards in coming years, perhaps triggering another baby boom. Although this wouldn't have an immediate impact on the supply of labour, it could help alleviate the problem further down the road.

Immigration policies that target younger workers could help to offset aging domestic workforces. But if, for whatever reasons, fulfilling the necessary immigration quota is ruled out, governments may have no option but to raise the normal retirement age. A recent study by the United Nations Population Division, *Replacement Migration: Is It a Solution to Declining and Ageing Populations?*, suggests that, in order to maintain the status quo without immigration, countries such as Great Britain and Italy would have to raise their retirement ages to 72 years and 77 years respectively. That's certainly food for thought.

The Ripple Effect of September 11

Unlikely though it may sound, the fallout from the September 11, 2001, terrorist attack on the World Trade Center in New York City could also leave its mark on the future retirement of many people.

The events of September 11 will significantly increase government spending, particularly in the areas of security and defence, possibly turning budget surpluses into budget deficits. This in turn could lead to higher interest rates and slow rates of economic growth in the future.

These unforeseen defence expenditures are now on a direct collision course with the unparalleled increases in old-age public pensions and health care costs that are slowly but relentlessly coming down the line. Cost-cutting exercises will have to come into play, and it is highly improbable that defence spending will be a likely candidate.

The terrorist attack also brought unprecedented scrutiny to potential immigrants, slowing down an already slow process and making future migration between countries and continents decidedly less feasible. This lessens the likelihood of immigration's being the answer to future workforce declines. In addition, the September 11 attack struck a devastating blow to the airline and travel industry, one that it may take years to recover from. These lost revenues will have an impact on government spending in the years to come.

Add to all of the above the significant declines over the past 18 months in the stock market, in which many Canadians have a good portion of their retirement savings socked away, and the stage is set for a major revision to many retirement plans. When all is said and done, we may all be very grateful if governments do raise the retirement age. In a perverse sense, it could be just the break we need.

Government Services under Siege? 2

*I*n *the early years of this country, Canada had no social security net or national health care system for its citizens. The ruling elite of that period in the country's history was, to put it mildly, strongly opposed to any such programs. The bottom line was that families were expected to take care of their own, with no help from the government purse. However, by 1927 the federal and provincial governments' attitudes had softened somewhat. Any Canadian who passed a means test (yes, they had them way back then) received an old age pension of $240 per year, or 66 cents a day. Anyone whose total annual income was more than $365 had it capped at that level. Evidently a dollar a day was considered more than adequate to live on.*

Over the years, through the continued and combined efforts of various federal and provincial governments, a national health care system was established, which has evolved into today's medicare. And when it comes to retirement income, Canadians now have access to a public pension system that includes Old Age Security (OAS), with its supplementary benefits for low-income seniors, and the Canada Pension Plan (CPP), with the Quebec Pension Plan (QPP) functioning as a parallel program. While there is no question that these programs have improved life for all Canadians, it's important to bear in mind that they were set up to operate in a very different landscape.

The number of Canadians over 65 years of age is expected to reach over 10 million by 2050. This will put considerable strain on existing health and social security programs. In addition — and this may be the real test, particularly of our public pension system — people are living longer. Back in the 1950s, when the average life expectancy was about 68 years, this was not an issue.

Today the average life expectancy for those who reach age 65 is about 82 years for men and 85 years for women. Whichever way you cut it, slice it, or dice it, that's an awful lot of additional years to fund. And that's today — given the continuing advances in medical health and research in microbiology and gene therapy, one can reasonably expect lifespans to be pushed to the upper limits. And these extended lifespans should become the norm for all future generations.

The question that remains is not so much whether existing health and social security programs will continue, but rather how will they change to adapt to these new realities. And how will these changes affect you?

Old Age Security: Will It Live Up to Its Name?

The OAS, which started in 1952, is funded out of general tax revenues. Along with the Guaranteed Income Supplement (GIS), it guarantees a basic, minimum level of income for all eligible elderly Canadians. The key word here is *minimum*. The OAS currently provides an annual maximum benefit of around $5,000 to every eligible senior, starting at 65 years of age — not by any means a princely amount. If you receive a full or partial OAS pension and have little or no other means of support — meaning that your annual income must fall below certain levels — you can also apply for the GIS. This would provide about an additional $4,000 a year.

Depending on how you look at these figures, you'll be either pleasantly surprised or rudely awakened. If it's the latter, it's worth remembering that OAS benefits were intended only to provide an income *floor* for beneficiaries; they were never meant to be a retiree's sole means of support. That having been said, though, it should be noted that one out of every three Canadians age 75 or older is currently living below the poverty line. Moreover, that floor is slowly developing cracks because of the clawback provisions introduced in 1989.

Under the clawback, or means test, you lose $150 in OAS benefits for every $1,000 of net annual income above the current threshold (about $55,000 for 2001). The pension is eliminated for those who have net annual incomes of more than $90,195. Although the clawback threshold and benefits are currently fully indexed to inflation — meaning that they will rise to keep pace with increases in the cost of living — there is no guarantee that this policy will continue. But these are peripheral issues. The fundamental question is, can the Old Age Security program withstand not only the growth of the 65+ age group, but also the unprecedented increases in lifespan? In other words, can the government afford to pay benefits to so many for so long? In two words, it depends.

The program could run into trouble if there were a substantial and continuing decrease in general tax revenues. Factors such as a steeper-than-projected decline in the workforce, low productivity, prolonged recession, and low immigration could result in various possible changes. In a worst-case scenario, the benefits could be lowered. However, as many elderly already live on fairly modest incomes, decreasing benefits would increase the poverty rate. Instead, changes might focus on lowering the clawback threshold or modifying the inflation factor. Either of these moves would mean smaller or no benefit payouts for an increasing number of future retirees. It's a possible future dilemma for the federal government. Would they raise income taxes to cover any shortfalls in the program, or would they completely abandon the so-called universality of the OAS?

Another option, of course, would be to change the eligibility age. This change has already been implemented in the United States, where they have instituted a phased-in program that will increase the normal retirement age for Social Security from 65 to 67 years of age. When you think about it, our federal government could make a good case for following suit. After all, they could argue, if life expectancies continue to creep ever upwards, the normal retirement age should rise accordingly, thereby delaying the date for receiving OAS benefits. At some time in the future, it could quite conceivably rise to age 70, or even beyond.

The Canada Pension Plan: A Program in Flux

The Canada and Quebec Pension Plans (C/QPP) were set up to provide income security to a contributor and his or her family upon retirement, disability, or death. The CPP operates in nine provinces and the territories, while the QPP operates in Quebec. Both plans are compulsory, contributory public pension plans covering Canadian workers age 18 to 70 who have annual earned incomes between $3,500 and the average industrial wage, which was $38,300 in 2001. While the maximum retirement benefit is currently around $9,300 a year, the average benefit paid out is considerably less: about $5,000.

In 1966, when the CPP was first introduced, it was designed so that benefits being paid out to seniors were financed largely from concurrent contributions being paid into the plan by workers and employers. At that time there were eight active workers to every one retiree, making this essentially pay-as-you-go system viable. The prospect of rapid growth in real wages and labour-force participation promised that the CPP would in all likelihood be sustained and remain affordable. It was expected that Canadians and their employers combined would never have to pay more than 5.5% of earnings towards the CPP.

Since those halcyon days, however, a great many things have changed. Escalating costs from improved benefits, lower contributions than originally expected because of the slowdown in wage and workforce growth, demographic change, and higher real interest rates have completely altered the circumstances in which the CPP is financed. By 1997, the ratio of workers to retirees had shrunk from eight contributors for every pensioner to five, and by 2030 there will be only three workers to support every pensioner.

Add the other curveball of extended lifespans, and you don't need to be an economics major to figure out that the plan was heading for rough water by the end of the 20th century. When federal and provincial governments reviewed the finances of the CPP in 1996, it was expected that contribution rates would have to rise to 10.1% by 2016 and then to 14.2% by 2030 — a 158% increase over the original 5.5%! But, even with these prodigious rate increases, the CPP reserve fund was expected to be empty by 2015. Given all of these factors, a pay-as-you-go system was obviously no longer an option.

To Market, to Market

With this dire outlook, new measures were legislated to shore up the finances of the CPP and ensure its future sustainability. These changes included the introduction of "steady-state" financing and the investment of the funds created by this type of financing in the marketplace to provide a higher rate of return. With steady-state financing, the long-term contribution rate is fixed at the lowest rate that will sustain the CPP indefinitely without any further increases. As a result, the combined employee/employer contribution rate will rise to 9.9% by 2003, where it will remain. In dollar terms, this means that an employee who earned the average wage of $38,300 or above in 2001 paid $1,496 (3.9%) in annual contributions. In 2003 that same employee will pay $1,722 for his or her share — an additional $18.83 a month.

The other initiative was the creation in 1998 of the CPP Investment Board (CPPIB) to manage and invest funds that are not needed by the plan to pay current pensions. When the board was first set up, it was essentially a passive investor; it could invest only in index funds — 80% in a fund that matched the performance of the TSE 300 Index and 20% in a fund that duplicated the Morgan Stanley Capital International Index.

In the CPPIB's first annual results, its equity portfolio delivered a stellar 40% return, which was due to the TSE 300's spectacular 43.3% performance. However, since Nortel at that time comprised about one-third of the TSE 300, this meant that about 25% of the board's assets were invested in one security. This was more than a little at odds with the board's policy of "maximizing returns without undue risk of loss." And, as the board's president, John MacNaughton, so aptly put it, "blindly following an indexation strategy has great potential risks to it." Consequently, the federal and provincial governments allowed the board to substantially reduce its portfolio weighting in Nortel holdings. Given that company's subsequent fall from grace in the fall of 2001 (from a high of over $120 per share to under $10), this was a move we should all be thankful for! But it does highlight the fund's new sensitivity to market fluctuations.

At the end of 2000, the CPP had total assets of about $41.6 billion. In addition to the approximately $6.4 billion of funds under management by the Investment Board, the CPP's assets include a portfolio of nearly $30 billion in provincial and federal government bonds, as well as a short-term operating reserve. Both the bond portfolio and the operating reserve are administered by the federal government, while the CPPIB manages all new monies paid into the plan.

The Board's Marching Orders

With these initiatives in place, the CPP will move away from pay-as-you-go financing to fuller funding, although not to the same extent as, say, a defined benefit plan. With a reserve of five years of benefits, the CPP will be only about 20% funded. This means that a large share of today's contributions will still be going towards paying the benefits of today's retirees. The total CPP account is projected to grow to approximately $100 billion by the end of 2007, of which between $70 billion and $90 billion would be available for management by the CPPIB.

Although the board has been set no specific investment target, the federal government's chief actuary has indicated that, in order to achieve long-term financial stability, the board needs to achieve a

4% real rate of return, to be combined with the 9.9% contribution rate hike. With an expected inflation rate of 3% annually, this would put the board's minimum long-term nominal target at 7%.

Doubts That Remain

But can these expectations be realized, and will these changes be sufficient to keep the fund viable? The creation of the Investment Board was not without its critics. Many question the wisdom of investing what will eventually be a significant portion of Canadians' retirement kitty in the stock market. Prolonged downturns and market meltdowns do occur. Japan comes to mind here. If the second-largest economy in the world can mire itself in a decades-long recession, can any country declare itself totally immune to such forces? Some people caution that the very size of the fund could eventually lead to a distortion in the market. Others fear low productivity growth and other political, economic, and demographic developments could jeopardize the sustainability of the plan. What if they prove to be right?

Well, even if they were proven right, we would not be looking at a total collapse of the public pension system. The result would probably be more in the nature of some additional fine-tuning, such as more contribution rate increases or erosion of some of the peripheral benefits — which, for many seniors, would be harmful enough. Other changes could include cutting core benefits by reducing the amount (currently 100%) that is indexed to inflation.

Since most other retirement income is not indexed to inflation, even those changes would mean a substantial and progressive decline in the standard of living of many elderly people. As with the OAS, the argument could also be made that longer lifespans should translate into later retirements, thereby smoothing the way to bump up the normal age for receiving benefits from 65 to 67 years of age, or even later.

Of course, any such proposed modifications would, without doubt, face opposition. Employees and employers alike may balk at further CPP rate increases, and cutting benefits either directly or indirectly would certainly meet fierce resistance from seniors, who, let's not forget, will have enormous political clout because of the growth in their numbers. The federal government may well find itself uncomfortably stuck between a rock and an extremely hard place.

Radical or Minor Surgery for Medicare?

In 1947 Saskatchewan, under the leadership of Premier Tommy Douglas, was the first province in Canada to provide public hospital insurance. By 1961 the residents of all 10 provinces and two territories had access to plans that provided comprehensive coverage for in-hospital care. By 1972 the plans had been extended to cover doctors' services outside hospitals. That, by all accounts, was the good old days.

Today it would appear that the public health service in many provinces is in dire need of restructuring. Who hasn't heard or read news reports about possibly life-threatening waits for treatment, lack of diagnostic equipment and technicians, overcrowded emergency rooms, overworked and underpaid medical professionals, and hospital closures? What's more, in a recent study, *Will the Baby Boomers Bust the Health Budget?*, the C.D. Howe Institute estimated that within 40 years, health spending will account for 57% of provincial budgets, an increase of 22% over current levels. And let's not forget those gloomy OECD predictions that Canada's health care spending will rise from about 6% of the GDP in 2000 to 10.5% in 2050.

When you look at demographics alone, with the senior population growing more than twice as fast as the overall population, the outlook for the future isn't promising. While the number of seniors in Canada is set to take a huge leap, the number of people in the workforce will shrink in relative terms. In 2000, the 20–64 age group made up close to 63% of the total population; by 2050, it will have dropped to under 55%. In sharp contrast, the 65+ age group, which was just under 13% of the total population in 2000, will increase dramatically to almost 25% in the year 2050.

This looming threat that a rapidly aging population will swamp the country's health care system, coupled with a potential decrease in tax revenues because of the relative decline in people in the workforce, has understandably brought forth loud cries for changes. These include moving to an outright two-tier system, user fees, and delisting of various services. Another option that has been floated is restricting medicare coverage to 75% of the cost of any medical service; the remaining 25% would have to be borne by individuals through private insurance. But bear in mind that these pessimistic predictions are based on some highly debatable suppositions. The most crucial of these is that people who are 65 and over will in the future continue to use the same quantity of health care services as older people have in the past. That supposition may be way off target.

Today, seniors not only live longer, but also live healthier for longer. This is in large part because of new drug treatments, such as those for high blood pressure, which have substantially improved the health of Canadians, making it possible for them to lead active, normal lives well into their 70s and 80s. This is a far cry from previous generations, when, as people aged, their health steadily deteriorated, often resulting in long, expensive stays in critical-care facilities. Considering that the improvement in Canadians' overall health is largely due to drug treatments, it is rather ironic that pharmaceuticals are not covered under medicare for the general public.

Opponents to a "pharmacare" program cite the huge costs associated with such a universal drug plan. Proponents argue that these costs could be balanced by the lower administrative expenditures of operating one plan as compared to many, and cheaper drugs because of greatly enhanced bargaining powers. According to the OECD report *Pharmaceutical Policies in OECD Countries: Reconciling Social and Industrial Goals*, only Canada, Mexico, Turkey, and the United States — out of some 29 industrialized nations — do not provide a universal drug plan.

In addition to new drug treatments, modern medical procedures (such as hip and knee replacements) have cut the average hospital stay dramatically. They have also enabled many other conditions to be treated in outpatient clinics, substantially reducing the cost of extended hospital stays. If this direction continues — and there is no reason why it shouldn't — many experts are anticipating that future demands on the health care system will be far less than those predicted by the C.D. Howe Institute and other similar studies. Indeed, that is the conclusion the provincial health ministers arrived at in a report prepared for their respective premiers. *Understanding Canada's Health Care Costs* predicts a 4.7% annual increase in provincial health care spending between 2000 and 2027, of which only 1% will be attributable to the health costs of seniors.

However, this does not mean that we can rest easy in retirement. Provincial budget deficits could translate into a re-evaluation of existing free prescription drug plans for seniors. Means testing is one method that could be employed, which would mean higher out-of-pocket expenses for many seniors. Also, many experts are anticipating a structural shift in health care, with lessening demand from those who are ill and an increasing need for care of the very elderly.

With seniors above the age of 80 now the fastest-growing segment of the population — a projected rise from 1 million in 2000 to 4 million in 2050 — this is a potential time bomb. In order to defuse the bomb, governments at all levels will have to provide more funding for in-home care and for the building of long-term care facilities. However, some seniors could be caught in the time lag between the inception and completion phases of any new initiatives. This would leave many of the very elderly and most vulnerable relying on family or nursing homes, with their high accompanying costs. According to the Spring 2001 edition of *IE: Money* magazine, an average stay of about two and a half years in an Ontario nursing home comes with a price tag of close to $100,000 — and that's for a government-subsidized facility.

Putting It All in Perspective

Any changes to our public pension and health care system, now or in the future, will have a profound effect on the vast majority of Canadians. Close to 95% of today's retirees receive benefits from the CPP and QPP, and these plans, combined with OAS and GIS, account for about 50% of seniors' income in Canada. Although these programs were never meant to be viewed as a sole source of retirement income, they are — for more than 25% of our senior citizens.

When it comes to health care, user fees or delisting of services currently covered by medicare could translate down the road into considerable out-of-pocket expenses for many seniors. In the United States, about a third of medical care expenditures for seniors are paid for privately, and it is estimated that health costs amount to close to 21% of family income for this age group.

The importance of Canada's public pension system as a foundation for providing income in retirement cannot be overstated. But it's prudent to keep in mind that the combined maximum benefits of OAS and the CPP will replace only up to about 40% of pre-retirement income, based on the average industrial wage, which is currently around $38,300. Unless you have additional sources of retirement income, you'll have to live on around $1,200 a month.

And don't make the mistakes of assuming that's what you will receive or doubling that amount if you are a working couple. Not every retiree is fortunate enough to receive the maximum CPP benefit of about $9,000 a year. Another point, but one that is often overlooked, is that many women will receive much smaller CPP benefits because of various factors, such as lower wages and prolonged absences from the workforce for child-rearing or looking after elderly parents.

Whichever way you look at, even if you are entitled to the maximum CPP and OAS benefits, unless you have other sources of retirement income, you will have to live for what could be a very long time on today's equivalent of around $14,500 a year. Now if this amount is adequate for your needs — great! But if it's not, and unless you intend to get back into the workforce, you could be faced with a severe and abrupt decline in your standard of living. And if the public pension net shrinks or health care costs increase, expect that drop to be even more precipitous. Think about it.

2

Facing the Retirement Income Challenge

3

An Uncertain Future

Not so many years ago, the vast majority of Canadians spent their entire working lives employed by the same company. On retirement they knew they could rely on receiving a monthly cheque for the rest of their lives for a specific dollar amount from the company's defined benefit pension plan. Come market slowdown, prolonged recession, or the occasional world crisis, retirees could unreservedly look forward to receiving these benefits month after month and year after year. What's more, high inflation followed by strong market demand also ensured soaring house prices, boosting the assets of many retirees far beyond their wildest expectations.

But what about tomorrow's retirees? Can they rely on receiving a specific retirement income, or will their standard of living be determined by unpredictable financial markets? Will they enjoy booming house prices, or should they, as some have predicted, anticipate a real estate market meltdown?

While the outcome of these questions will undoubtedly influence your retirement lifestyle, they are mere blips on life's radar screen when compared with the unprecedented challenge of living far longer than any generation that has gone before. Gone are the days when the vast majority of Canadians retired at age 65 and died not long thereafter. The true challenge will be dealing with the new reality — that a great many of us will live well into our 90s or, quite possibly, given the scope and acceleration of medical advances in *this area, reach 100 and beyond. Will individuals rise to this "centenarian challenge" or fall victim to it?*

How Long Will I Live?

As mentioned in Chapter 1, the vast majority of men today who reach the age of 65 will die between 74 and 94 years of age, while women tend to die between 77 and 96. For a male, this means you may have to fund as few as nine years of retirement or as many as 29. And for a female, you may have to fund 12 years or as many as 31. Of course, there is also no guarantee that you won't be one of the approximately 30% who die earlier or live to become a centenarian. In other words, determining your life expectancy is a guessing game with no definitive answer.

To get some idea on your likely life expectancy, it's important to look at lifespans within your own family. If your relatives are living well into their late 80s or 90s, then chances are you will too. If they typically die in their 60s or 70s, then a visit to your family doctor would not be remiss. While you can't alter your genes — not yet, anyway — preventive medicine can and does help lengthen lifespans. To get a handle on how long you might live, you can also complete a quiz on the Internet at <www.livingto100.com>.

How healthy you are in your retirement will also play a key role in assessing how long your nest egg will last. If you succumb to some debilitating disease, the associated health care costs will eat into your savings. And, if we do move more towards a two-tier system as some are suggesting, we could be looking at substantial out-of-pocket health care expenses. In the United States, where about a third of medical care expenditures for seniors are paid for privately, it is estimated that health costs amount to about $4 out of every $10 of family income for this age group. On the other hand, retirees who are healthy tend to spend more on travel and leisure activities, such as golf. Many retirees, providing their health holds up, typically don't slow down and consequently spend less until around the 80-year mark.

When trying to figure out how long you are likely to live and how much you are going to need, it's wise to assume that you will live for a longer time rather than a shorter one. That way, if you do get to become a member of the century club, you will still have the cash to indulge in a gala birthday bash. The alternative is not an attractive option.

The Shift in Company Pension Plans

Although, for the moment, defined benefit (DB) plans are still the most common type of pension plan for large, well-established corporations and government, newer companies are passing them by in favour of defined contribution (DC) plans. While this type of plan is certainly more amenable to the reality of today's mobile workplace, it also shifts the responsibility for providing retirement income away from the employer and onto the employee. In other words, employers are not committed to paying their employees a specific amount at retirement. This means that, unlike in previous generations, the incomes of many future retirees will rest entirely in their own hands.

Unlike the defined benefit plan, with its retirement guarantee of a monthly cheque for a specific amount for life, the actual dollar amount of a DC plan is not known until the day you retire. On top of that, your retirement income from this final amount will depend on prevailing market conditions at the time you retire, your future investment choices, and the return on your invested money. You might end up way ahead of a typical DB plan benefit, but then again, you could end up a lot worse off. This unpredictability makes retirement income projections a lot more uncertain.

Still, to be fair, DC plans do have their advantages. When you die, your beneficiaries or your estate gets the remaining lump sum. With a DB, there is no lump sum for your heirs to inherit. Even if you die the day after you retire, your spouse or any other eligible dependants would receive only reduced payments. But for many future retirees, a DB plan, with its guarantee of a cheque for a specific amount every month for what could be a very long retirement, might outweigh any other considerations — especially if their other sources of retirement income are unsure.

Demographics and the Stock Market

The popular hypothesis is that demographics — the science of human populations — is the primary driving force behind stock market movements. If we accept that the baby boomers have driven the markets up, then it would seem rational to assume that when they retire and sell off their holdings, they will drive the markets down. While that sounds quite logical, there are a number of factors that will act to mitigate a stock market meltdown as the boomers begin to retire around 2010.

One would naturally expect that, as the boomers hit retirement, they will take money out of the stock market or move some of their assets to more conservative investments, such as bonds. But, because of increasing lifespans, the baby boomers will have to manage a retirement that could stretch to 30 years or more. That means they'll probably have to keep at least part of their retirement savings in the stock market for many years to come. Second, let's not forget that the boomers will not all stop working on the same day, but will retire over a 20- to 30-year span, further ensuring that any sell-off of stocks will be watered down.

And finally, another factor that will mute the boomers' influence will be the gradual infusion of monies into the market from the Canada Pension Plan account. These investments are projected to total the not insignificant amount of between $70 billion and $90 billion by the end of 2007, just as the first wave of boomers starts to retire. In addition, if interest rates continue at their current historical lows, fixed-income investments will not be an attractive alternative.

Even if the baby-boom generation does pull away from stocks, it is highly unlikely that this alone would be enough to cause a market meltdown. Monetary and fiscal policies, the health of our economy and that of our neighbours, stable political climates, technological innovation, and consumer and investor confidence are just some of the other factors that together exert a much stronger force.

But there is no denying that a major sell-off by the boomers would have, at the very least, a dampening effect on the stock market, and at the other end of the spectrum, could exert a pernicious influence on pre-existing negative market conditions. One can imagine retirees panicking and cashing out of stocks if the market suffers prolonged double-digit declines. And who could blame them? It's one thing to hang on during market turbulence when you have a regular paycheque coming in, but it's quite another when you are in your 70s, 80s, or 90s and depending on your investments to pay your living expenses. To add to this uncertainty, retirees will also need to focus on, and come to terms with, the very real possibility of achieving much more modest returns in the future.

Lower Stock Market Returns

As we all know, or should know, the total return from holding a stock comes from two sources: dividends and capital gains. Over the past 50 years, the dividend yield from the S&P 500 index has averaged about 4% and has typically accounted for about 40% of the index's total return, which is around 11%. Today, however, the dividend yield is at a record low of around 1.5%. In addition, although stock prices can and do fluctuate significantly in the short term, returns from capital gains cannot grow faster than the long-term rate of growth of the economy. So what does this mean for future stock market returns?

As a rough estimate, assuming a dividend yield of between 1.5% and 2% and projecting a real (inflation-adjusted) long-term rate of growth of the economy of between 2.5% and 3%, this would imply that future stock market real returns will be in the region of 4% to 5%. Factoring in a 3% rate of inflation, which corresponds to the long-term historical average for North America, this means that investors could be looking to the stock market to deliver a nominal rate of return of about 7% to 8%, well below the long-term average of 10% to 11%.

While no one can predict the future, it would seem prudent to base one's financial plans on the stock market's returning less in the future. That way, any upswing would be a bonus.

A Real Estate Bust?

Most of us are well aware of the boom and bust theories associated with the baby boomer generation and the real estate market. Depending on whom you listen to, we could be headed for a real estate meltdown between now and 2010; the housing supply is expected to exceed demand because of a decline in new family formation brought about by an aging population. This dire prediction is based on the premise that demography is the key element in forecasting trends in just about everything, including house prices.

If you are a demographics devotee, then you believe that the baby-boom generation, those born between 1946 and 1964, drives everything from the stock market to increases or decreases in tie sales. You will also be of the opinion that when the baby boomers start retiring around 2010, housing prices will free fall. This expectation is based on the hypothesis that the vast majority of retirees will want to sell their homes and, because of the "birth dearth" between 1967 and 1979, there will be nobody to buy them.

Of course, all this rests on a theoretical model based on the science of demography alone. No weight is given to other crucial factors, such as economic growth, fiscal and monetary policy, or the effects of inflation and immigration. A study titled *Demographic Changes and Real Housing Prices in Canada*, funded by the Canadian Mortgage and Housing Corporation (CMHC), determined that the contention of real price decrease becomes plausible only in a scenario with weak economic growth, low fertility, and low levels of immigration. And even then, the decrease would be small. The study concluded that, if it is true that demographics may exert downward pressure on real estate prices, such an impact would probably be dominant only in certain regions, depending even there on their rates of growth in real income. In other regions, the real price should tend to rise.

So what does this all mean for the average homeowners who may be contemplating selling their house on retirement? One important point to keep in mind is that not every retiree will want to sell his or her home. According to the May 1997 issue of *Mobility* magazine, more than half of homeowners age 65 and over had lived for 20+ years in their homes, and three out of 10 had done so for 30+ years. And although demographics may indeed exert downward pressure on the real estate market in certain areas of the country, many other key economic factors can and will either exacerbate or alleviate the situation. However, one can expect this debate to continue, which — depending on who gets the most media coverage — can only serve to make any retirement plans a little less sure.

Looking Ahead

So what does all this mean? Quite simply, it means increased uncertainty for tomorrow's retirees. Given the move away from defined benefit plans, the retirement savings of many Canadians will now be vulnerable to stock market volatility and their future incomes will be less secure. When it comes to real estate, with the Bank of Canada's commitment to low inflation targets and other factors, it may be prudent to assume that although your home may be your castle, its worth may not increase quite as much as you might like. What's more, your retirement savings may have to last another 20, 30, or even 40 years.

One fact that has been driven home to most Canadians — courtesy of their monthly statements — is that stock markets go up and down. So wealth, particularly in the case of stock market bubbles, can be a fragile and transitory state. One month you have it, the next month you don't. In order to create wealth, there are really only two possible paths that we can take. We can build wealth either through capital appreciation or through increased savings. As we have little control over capital gains, it would seem prudent to focus on the one area over which we have complete power: our ability to save more. Ultimately, simplistic though it may sound, how much we save and how much we spend may be the two factors that will determine our future retirement lifestyles.

How Much Is Enough?

*M*ention the word "retirement" to most people and you will get a wide range of responses. Some view their future retirement with pleasurable anticipation, as a time for personal fulfillment. Others dread the mere thought of it and intend to keep working as long as possible. Whichever camp you fall into — and many of us vacillate between the two — you will eventually have to give some thought to various questions: Where will you live? How will you fill your time? and most important of all, How much money will you need?

Are You Saving Enough for Retirement?

Pension organizations have issued a number of warnings — so far, mostly ignored — that many people could face shortfalls on their retirement pensions. According to the Association of Consulting Actuaries (ACA) in Britain, if you are starting to save for retirement at age 25, you will need to put aside 10% to 15% of your annual salary. At age 30, you will need to save 12% to 17%, and at age 35, 15% to 20%. If you delay until you are 45 years old, the amount you will need to save becomes an impractical 23% to 30%.

Of course, working Canadians pay into the Canada or Quebec Pension Plan (C/QPP). But even if you were paying the maximum contribution of 4.3% in 2001, this, coupled with your employer's equal contribution, would amount to only 8.6% — 1.4% below the minimum 10% recommended by the ACA for a 25-year-old.

Because the maximum contribution to the C/QPP is tied to maximum pensionable earnings ($38,300 for 2001), not your annual income, the shortfall gets larger for higher wage earners. For someone earning $75,000, it amounts to a savings shortfall of close to 4.5% of annual income, and at a salary of $100,000, the savings shortfall reaches almost 7%.

If we use the ACA's percentages as a guideline to achieving an adequate retirement income, many middle-to-higher-income earners, unless they are saving substantial amounts elsewhere, will face significant shortfalls on their pensions. And, according to a recent Statistics Canada survey, it appears this will indeed be the case. The report found that 41% of family units with incomes of $75,000 or more might not be able to replace two-thirds of their pre-retirement earnings. This means that the day they retire, their annual incomes will drop by close to 35%!

The standard rule of thumb is to maintain the purchasing power of 65% to 85% of your pre-retirement income. This means that if your current salary is $60,000, you would need an annual retirement income of between $39,000 and $51,000. Depending on the type of retirement lifestyle you envisage, you might need much less or much more. But you won't know unless you sit down and give it some thought. The Retirement Expenses Worksheet in Appendix B is a great way to get started. However, to determine how much money will be enough to fund the type of retirement lifestyle you wish, it is becoming increasingly important to recognize that we can no longer contemplate retirement as a strictly monolithic entity.

It is quite possible that your retirement could last 30 or 40 years — almost a lifetime in itself (which it would have been if you lived in medieval England). Therefore, when contemplating retirement, perhaps it's best to think of it in three distinct stages, the first stage lasting from 65 to 75 years of age, the second from around 75 to 85, and the third from 85 years of age.

The First Stage: Funding an Active Retirement

In the first, or active, stage of retirement, typically from 65 to 75 years of age, some of us will continue to work on either a full-time or part-time basis. Preferably this will be out of choice rather than necessity. In the early stage of retirement, many people hope to fulfill dreams of extensive travel and staying at world-class hotels, or of going to the theatre. None of these activities comes cheap. In nominal terms, over the decade from 1990 to 2000, average American consumer prices increased by 29%, at an annual rate of 2.6%. But those hotel rooms and theatre tickets increased by about 80% and 75% respectively over the same 10-year period. If either of these pastimes coincides with your plans, you had better ensure that you are saving adequately for them.

For those with a yen to cruise the Islands, you're in luck. This activity costs less than it did a decade ago. And if you plan to lead a fairly quiet lifestyle, your income needs will obviously be lower. But even so, with about 2,000 extra hours of free time on your hands every year, you may find yourself taking up new leisure activities, some of which can be expensive. If golf is your game, you're looking at paying anywhere between $1,500 and $10,000 to cover two rounds a week for about six months of the year.

On the plus side, you won't have any work-related costs such as business clothes, commuting expenses, and paying into a pension plan or employment insurance. But many couples who delayed starting their families until later in life may have children who require some financial support or, like some, may still be paying off a mortgage.

The Second Stage: Slow and Steady

The years from 75 to 85 could be considered the second, or settled, stage of retirement. During this period, your outlays could decline by 20% or more, as many retirees prefer to stay nearer to home and lead a less active lifestyle. Health-related costs, however, could now start to become an issue. As increased numbers of baby boomers flood the public health system, many retirees may (depending on how you view the future of our health care system) have to choose between lengthy waits for treatment or paying privately. Choose the latter and you could be looking at bills ranging from $25,000 for chemotherapy, and anywhere from $40,000 to $140,000 for bypass surgery. What's more, a growing number of retirees may find they have to pay a larger share of their medical and dental expenses, costs previously covered by their former employers.

Furthermore, 10 or 20 years into your retirement, inflation — if not factored into your original retirement income equation — will have gradually eroded your purchasing power. Could you afford, for example, to remain in your apartment if the rent rose from $900 to $1,350 over a 10-year period, a 50% increase? Many retirees can't. They are forced to move to cheaper accommodations, often in a new location far from their old neighbourhood.

The Third Stage: The Costs of Being Old

Many retirees once they reach age 85 and older face increased medical costs and, depending on their health and circumstances, decisions regarding retirement residences and nursing homes. All of these factors could result in a major jump in expenses. Prices in privately run retirement residences typically range from $800 for shared accommodation to as much as $7,000 per month for a private suite. Not-for-profit retirement residences often have subsidies and rent that is geared to income, which sounds ideal, but there's a catch. With rents often in the $1,000-per-month range, these facilities usually have long waiting lists that can delay residency for up to two or three years.

By 2030, when the boomers are entering their 70s and 80s, these waiting lists will lengthen, and prices for privately run retirement residences could escalate dramatically if demand outstrips supply. Government agencies will undoubtedly be looking at extending existing programs and funding for new facilities, but many retirees could be caught in the time lag between the inception and completion phase of any new initiatives.

As retirement residences cater only to individuals in relatively good health, retirees with serious physical or mental problems will have to rely on extended hospital care or private nursing homes, with their accompanying costs. A study by the U.S. Department of Health and Human Services shows that people at 65 years of age face at least a 40% lifetime chance of entering a nursing home. About 10% stay there five years or longer. In 1991, according to Health Canada, men age 65 and older could expect to have severe disabilities during their last two years, and women for their last four years of life.

In this respect, seniors living in Ontario could be particularly hard hit, facing a bill of close to $100,000 for the average two-and-a-half-year stay in a government-subsidized nursing facility. Generally speaking, the farther west one goes from Ontario, the larger the portion of the bill the government picks up. The possibility of footing nursing-home bills may sway many retirees towards long-term care (LTC) insurance to help cover the costs of home or institutional care. As always, premiums and coverage varies among providers, so if you decide to go this route, shop around. As a ball-park figure, you're currently looking at payments of around $200 a month for men at age 65, and about $300 for women.

A Movable Line

The stages of retirement are, of course, not set in stone. Many retirees will live active, healthy lives until the day they die. Others may require extended nursing care starting early in retirement. As we have no way of knowing what the future holds for us, perhaps it's best to simply prepare for the worst and hope for the best. Take an objective look at your own and your immediate family's medical history to decide whether or not you need insurance coverage for long-term care or nursing home needs. You can expect to hear a lot more about these insurance products in the coming years.

Do You Have a Retirement Income Gap?

Your retirement income gap is the shortfall between your projected retirement income, based on the dollar amount currently accumulated, and your retirement income goal. In other words, it's the difference between what you have and what you would like to have. For some of us, the gap may be either trivial or overwhelmingly large. If it's the latter, and many of us may be in that position, despite the so-called "baby boomer wealth effect," don't throw in the towel. Simply taking the step of identifying the dollar amount of your retirement income gap has proven to be a powerful motivator.

Get Motivated

According to a recent survey of retirement confidence by the non-partisan Employee Benefits Research Institute and the American Savings Education Council, six out of 10 individuals who had actually completed their retirement income needs calculation were on track to meeting their retirement goals. In sharp contrast, seven out of 10 Americans who had not done the calculation felt that they were well behind schedule. Of those who had done the calculation to determine what their retirement gap was going to be, over half of them had altered their savings behaviour. Fifty-four percent had started to save more for their retirement, and one out of four had changed the asset allocations of their investments.

Determining your retirement income gap is probably the most

important step any future retiree can take, and it's crucial to achieving your retirement income goals. To plan for a future in which our public pension and health care systems may be strained to their limits, our private pensions are uncertain, and we may live in retirement for one year or 40, we need to take a look at some hard numbers.

Doing the Numbers

Let's assume you are 55 years of age, planning to retire at age 65, are mortgage free, and have a 30-year retirement income goal of $40,000. The first step is to determine what income you will receive from Old Age Security (OAS) and the Canada or Quebec Pension Plan (C/QPP). In this example, we have assumed the current maximum annual payout of around $5,000 from OAS and the maximum of about $9,000 from the C/QPP. This gives you a total income of around $14,000 from the public pension system (see Table 5a).

Table 5a

Identifying Your Retirement Income Gap

1. Annual Retirement income goal		$ 40,000
2. Sources of Income		
OAS	$ 5,000	
CPP	$ 9,000	
Company pension	$ 16,000	
Total income		$ 30,000
3. Retirement income gap (line 1 – line 2)		$ 10,000
4. Total assets needed at retirement to generate income of $10,000 (see Table 5b)		$ 166,766
5. Amount already saved in RRSPs, other investments, etc.		$ 60,000
6. Value of current savings at retirement (see Table 5c: $60,000 x 2.16)		$ 129,600
7. Asset shortfall at retirement (line 4 – line 6)		$ 18,424
8. Annual savings needed to reach retirement income goal of $40,000 (see Table 5d)		**$ 1,324**

It's important at this point to insert a word of caution. Don't automatically assume that because you have been working since you were 20, you will receive the maximum payout. In order to be eligible for this amount you would need to work for 40 years and to pay the maximum C/QPP contribution each and every year. Check your Statement of Contributions for the amount of your projected retirement pension.

The next step is to include any company pension plans such as defined benefit (DB), defined contribution (DC), and group registered retirement savings plans (group RRSPs). As a member of a DB plan, our future retiree can count on receiving a guaranteed pension income of $16,000 a year. Again, be cautious here. The retirement income received from some DB plans, unlike our example, includes all eligible C/QPP benefits. Check yours out using the Company Pension Plan Questionnaire in Appendix A.

With a total projected income of $30,000 and an income goal of $40,000, this leaves a retirement income gap of $10,000. To provide this income and to be able to retire in 10 years, additional savings of $166,766 will be needed (see Table 5b, line 2, column 2). Table 5b also clearly illustrates the effects of inflation — in this case, 3%, the historical average — on the value of your dollar over time. In order to obtain an annual retirement income of $50,000 in five years, one would need $719,270. However, taking inflation into account, someone planning to retire in 40 years would need over $2,000,000 to generate the same retirement income of $50,000.

Our future retiree has already accumulated $60,000 in his RRSP, which, assuming an 8% rate of return, will be worth $129,600 on retirement (see Table 5c, line 2, column 4: $60,000 x 2.16). This leaves him with an asset shortfall of $18,424. In order to meet his retirement income goal of $40,000 a year, he needs to save approximately $1,361 every year for the next 10 years (see Table 5d, line 1, column 2 [$75 x 8.5 = $637] plus line 2, column 2 [$724]).

Tables 5b and 5d assume a 30-year retirement, with a zero balance at the end of the 30 years. Because of the inherent dangers associated with future values based on averages, these results should

Table 5b

Total Amount Needed at Retirement

If your income shortfall is:	Years to Retirement							
	5	10	15	20	25	30	35	40
$ 5,000	$ 71,927	$ 83,383	$ 96,664	$ 112,060	$ 129,908	$ 150,600	$ 174,586	$ 202,393
10,000	143,854	166,766	193,328	224,120	259,816	301,200	349,172	404,786
15,000	215,781	250,149	289,992	336,180	389,724	451,800	523,758	607,179
20,000	287,708	333,532	386,656	448,240	519,632	602,400	698,344	809,572
25,000	359,635	416,915	483,320	560,300	649,540	753,000	872,930	1,011,965
30,000	431,562	500,298	579,984	672,360	779,448	903,600	1,047,516	1,214,358
40,000	575,416	667,064	773,312	896,480	1,039,264	1,204,800	1,396,688	1,619,144
50,000	719,270	833,830	966,640	1,120,600	1,299,080	1,506,000	1,745,860	2,023,930

(assumes 7% compound annual return and annual inflation of 3%)

Table 5c

Factor to Determine Future Value of Savings

Years to Goal	Rate of Return					
	5%	6%	7%	8%	9%	10%
5	1.28	1.34	1.40	1.47	1.54	1.61
10	1.63	1.79	1.97	2.16	2.37	2.59
15	2.08	2.40	2.76	3.17	3.64	4.18
20	2.65	3.21	3.87	4.66	5.60	6.73
25	3.39	4.29	5.43	6.85	8.62	10.83
30	4.32	5.74	7.61	10.06	13.27	17.45
35	5.52	7.69	10.68	14.79	20.41	28.10
40	7.04	10.29	14.97	21.72	31.41	45.26

be viewed as strictly ballpark figures (see Chapter 6 for more on this subject).

Facing the Gap

Completing the worksheet in Appendix C will help you determine whether or not you are going to have a retirement income shortfall. You may find that you are in the enviable position of having reached your goal. Does that mean you should stop saving? That's up to you. But surplus money never hurt anyone, and it's a great stress reliever when faced with the unexpected, such as a forced early retirement or disappointing investment returns.

If, on the other hand, you have identified that you are not going to achieve your retirement income goal unless you start saving more, you have a dilemma. Either you cut back now or you cut back later. You have the luxury of that choice now, but make the wrong decision and, like many retirees, you won't have that indulgence later. According to a poll conducted by Compas for the CIBC, over one-third (38%) of retired Canadians reported that they lack sufficient savings to maintain the lifestyle they had envisioned for their retirement years. Still, if you do have a gap (which will probably be the case for many people), don't give up.

Table 5d

Annual Savings Needed to Reach Retirement Income Goal

If your savings shortfall is:	Years to Retirement							
	5	10	15	20	25	30	35	40
$ 1,000	$ 174	$ 75	$ 40	$ 24	$ 16	$ 11	$ 7	$ 5
10,000	1,739	724	398	244	158	106	72	50
25,000	4,347	1,809	995	610	395	265	181	125
50,000	8,694	3,618	1,990	1,220	790	530	362	250
75,000	13,041	5,427	2,985	1,830	1,185	795	543	375
100,000	17,388	7,236	3,980	2,440	1,580	1,060	724	500
150,000	26,082	10,854	5,970	3,660	2,370	1,590	1,086	750
200,000	34,776	14,472	7,960	4,880	3,160	2,120	1,448	1,000
250,000	43,470	18,090	9,950	6,100	3,950	2,650	1,810	1,250
300,000	52,164	21,708	11,940	7,320	4,740	3,180	2,172	1,500
400,000	69,552	28,944	15,920	9,760	6,320	4,240	2,896	2,000
500,000	86,940	36,180	19,900	12,200	7,900	5,300	3,620	2,500

(assumes 7% compound annual return)

There Are Always Options

Don't assume you can't possibly put away any more money for your retirement. There are many relatively painless ways of finding those additional dollars. Eliminating one cup of coffee a day puts about $350 a year back in your pocket. Going to the hairstylist every five weeks instead of every four could help you retain anywhere from $75 to $500 over a 12-month period. To save larger amounts, consider postponing a major purchase, such as keeping the car for an additional year or two before buying a new model.

If you had been planning to retire at 55 or 60 years of age, you can delay your retirement to give you some extra years to put away more assets. Or, to give you that additional income and still retire as planned, you could rethink your retirement to include part-time work. Many seniors are re-entering the workforce by either returning to their original professions or seeking new opportunities in different areas of employment. Given the birth dearth and low immigration, many sectors may experience sharp declines in their labour forces in the future. These industries could have to re-evaluate their hiring and retirement policies to include older workers and more flexible working arrangements.

Another alternative might be to reallocate your investment mix to increase the growth on your retirement savings. If your money is sitting in money market funds or GICs, you won't be getting much of a bang for your buck. Over the past five years, the average Canadian money market fund has delivered 3.7%, and five-year GICs, 4.8%. Granted they are safe, but if you need that additional growth and you have a time horizon of more than five years, putting some — not all — of your assets into equities could get you closer to your goal. To determine the best route for you, it's best to get qualified professional advice.

If you have an unbridgeable retirement income gap, there are three possible reasons why. It could be that your retirement income goal is unrealistic, that you have procrastinated too long, or that you are unwilling to make compromises. When it comes to retirement income, let's face it — bar winning a lottery, it's probably chancy for many of us to hope to attain six figures plus. It's probably also unwise to expect to reach your goal if you have left it to the last minute or if you refuse to change any aspect of your retirement income plan. If you fall into either of those categories, let's hope it's the latter. At least there you still have the opportunity to turn things around. As for the other, perhaps buying a lottery ticket isn't such a bad idea after all.

The Trouble with Averages

6

*M*ost *people like dealing with averages, especially when it comes to their investments. Averages provide an uncomplicated yardstick on which to base financial decisions and potential future returns. Comparisons can easily be made between different investments by looking at their respective "average" annualized compound returns over any given period. Although the year-to-year results won't match the average return, averages give investors insight into which investments — be they bonds, stocks, or a particular mutual fund — might help them reach their long-term financial goals. But when it comes to projecting future retirement income flows, relying solely on these averages as a gauge can be highly misleading.*

A False Sense of Stability

The average annual compound return for the TSE 300 Index over the past 25 years (from 1975 to 2000) was 9.3% — not too bad. Most retirees would be happy with that return over the long term. However, they would not be too pleased with the fluctuations in year-to-year results and how those variations would have affected their flow of retirement income. Figure 6a plots the yearly highs and lows the TSE 300 Index encountered along the way. They're not too much of a worry when you're saving for retirement, but an entirely different proposition when you want a stable flow of income.

Figure 6a

Fluctuations in the TSE 300 Index, 1975–2000

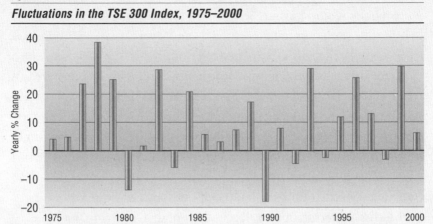

A Cautionary Tale

There are hundreds of retirement income calculators on the Internet, and most of us have used them at one time or another. Many of them work on the same principle: You simply punch in your starting balance at retirement and your expected annual rate of return, and select the number of years you want your money to last. Then you click on "submit" and, presto, you know whether you'll be eating caviar or dog food. Of course, if you don't like the result, you can always increase the expected rate of return — immediately your retirement lifestyle will take on a more golden hue.

Regardless of the assumptions made, these calculators typically show a steady, dependable stream of annual income and a gradually declining year-end balance. It doesn't matter whether you assume a 5% or 25% annual rate of return, or a 10-, 20-, or 30-year retirement time span. It doesn't matter whether your starting balance is $60,000, $100,000, or $600,000. Naturally, the stream of income will be higher or lower depending on the assumptions made, but the final assertion will still be the same, namely, that you will receive a fixed stream of retirement income and that it will last the required number of years.

Therein lies the danger. In order to replicate this in real time, your money would have to be in an investment that is guaranteed to deliver the same annual return each and every year, and continue to do so over the entire retirement period.

Generally speaking, most investments don't deliver a nice steady, fixed 8% or 10% each and every year. While their 10-, 20-, or 30-year average annual return may indeed be 8% or 10%, their yearly returns will fluctuate, sometimes dramatically. To bring this point home, Table 6a compares projected retirement income streams based on a typical retirement calculator with those generated from two actual mutual funds, a balanced fund and an equity fund.

In this illustration we have assumed a starting balance of $100,000, a 30-year retirement period, a 9% average annual rate of return over the entire term, and an end balance of zero. Both the balanced fund and the equity fund delivered an average annual compound return of 9% over a 30-year period.

What You See May Not Be What You Get

As you will see, the results based on using a retirement calculator run true to form, with no surprises. With a starting balance of $100,000 and assuming a 9% average annual rate of return, it determines that you will be able to withdraw $9,360 every year for the entire 30-year period. Furthermore, this would be accomplished with only gradual declines in the year-end balance. No uncertainties there, but when you tie the same withdrawals to actual fund data, it's a very different story.

In the case of the balanced fund, you would have run out of money in your 21st year of retirement, and when you take a look at the equity fund, you would barely have made it into your 17th year. Even the dog food goes out the window there. What's more, while the calculator estimated total annual withdrawals of close to $281,000, the funds actually provided far less. Also, although each fund delivered the required average annual compound rate of return of 9% over the entire 30-year period, their annual returns ranged

Table 6a

Determining Future Retirement Income Streams:
The Dangers of Using Retirement Calculators

Year	9% Fixed Rate of Return*		Balanced Fund**		Equity Fund**	
	Year-end Withdrawal	Annual Balance	Year-end Withdrawal	Annual Balance	Year-end Withdrawal	Annual Balance
1	$ 9,360	$ 99,266	$ 9,360	$ 107,780	$ 9,360	$ 70,960
2	9,360	98,467	9,360	102,870	9,360	79,471
3	9,360	97,595	9,360	68,557	9,360	80,323
4	9,360	96,645	9,360	72,052	9,360	77,998
5	9,360	95,609	9,360	72,646	9,360	63,554
6	9,360	94,481	9,360	61,618	9,360	59,670
7	9,360	93,250	9,360	61,027	9,360	52,425
8	9,360	91,909	9,360	65,748	9,360	42,507
9	9,360	90,447	9,360	67,062	9,360	37,903
10	9,360	88,854	9,360	54,750	9,360	42,721
11	9,360	87,117	9,360	47,860	9,360	42,913
12	9,360	85,224	9,360	60,842	9,360	40,324
13	9,360	83,161	9,360	51,580	9,360	20,162
14	9,360	80,911	9,360	46,837	9,360	21,793
15	9,360	78,460	9,360	42,894	9,360	10,744
16	9,360	75,788	9,360	42,963	9,360	3,050
17	9,360	72,875	9,360	31,037	3,022	0
18	9,360	69,700	9,360	26,405	0	0
19	9,360	66,239	9,360	14,903	0	0
20	9,360	62,467	9,360	7,698	0	0
21	9,360	58,356	8,056	0	0	0
22	9,360	53,874	0	0	0	0
23	9,360	48,989	0	0	0	0
24	9,360	43,664	0	0	0	0
25	9,360	37,860	0	0	0	0
26	9,360	31,534	0	0	0	0
27	9,360	24,639	0	0	0	0
28	9,360	17,123	0	0	0	0
29	9,360	8,930	0	0	0	0
30	9,360	0	0	0	0	0
Total	**$ 280,800**		**$ 195,256**		**$ 152,782**	

Annual dollar withdrawals assume a starting balance of 100,000, a 9% average annual rate of return over a 30-year period for each investment category, and an ending balance of zero.
* Results based on using a typical retirement calculator to project future income stream.
** Projected retirement income stream using actual mutual fund returns. Both funds posted an average annual compound return of 9% over a 30-year period.

from a high of 49.4% to a low of –25.8% for the balanced fund, and from 65.9% to –30.9% for the equity fund.

Neither fund actually delivered a 9% return in any one of the 30 years. Moreover, over the relevant 30-year period, the balanced fund experienced seven years of negative growth, while the equity fund chalked up nine years in negative territory. This meant that their year-end balances bounced around — a lot harder to live with.

Why the difference in results between the calculator and the two funds? Retirement calculators assume that the money will grow essentially in a straight line, in this case, at a constant 9% rate of return every year over a 30-year period. They do not consider variations in returns. As you can see, that's not the way it happens. Yearly returns do fluctuate, and if you are withdrawing a fixed amount, you eat into more of your principal when your investments take a hit. This in turn lessens the ability of your nest egg to grow to provide for future years.

What does this mean for retirees? Simply that caution should be exercised when using average annualized compound rates of return and retirement calculators to predict future income flows. While these tools can be helpful in projecting your future retirement savings, they can be unreliable when trying to plan for a secure income in retirement.

7

Facing the Unpredictable

Bull markets are great — especially when you're heading into retirement, when continued double-digit returns can make a phenomenal difference in the net worth of your accumulated nest egg. Bear markets are, of course, quite a different story. They're the last thing anyone holding significant assets in the stock market wants to experience at or near the eve of their retirement. The prospect of your future retirement income being wiped out by month after month of relentless declines is enough to cause panic in even the most stalwart investor.

But are these fears simply an understandable overreaction to negative market conditions? Are these apprehensions groundless, or are they to some degree mitigated by nation-states' vigilant monetary and fiscal policies and the technological innovations that now control or "curb" the volume of trades? Does it in fact make any significant difference to future income flows whether your retirement coincides with a bull or a bear market?

How Bull and Bear Markets Affect Retirement Incomes

The following illustration uses actual mutual fund data to show clearly how retirement income streams in the first five years of retirement were affected by two very different market conditions, the 1973–74 bear market and the subsequent bull market that began in September 1974. (During the 1973–74 bear market, the TSE 300 shed 34% over 11 months.) All the portfolios assume a starting balance of $100,000, with an annual withdrawal rate of 5%.

Table 7a

Retirement Incomes and Bear Markets

	100% Equities		50% Equities/50% Bonds		100% Bonds	
Year	Annual Income	Year-end Balance	Annual Income	Year-end Balance	Annual Income	Year-end Balance
1	$ 3,760	$ 60,300	$ 4,240	$ 75,050	$ 4,750	$ 91,800
2	3,370	63,900	4,075	80,000	4,790	96,900
3	3,785	72,100	4,470	88,700	5,090	104,900
4	3,695	73,800	4,610	92,900	5,525	112,200
5	4,515	98,600	5,760	107,950	5,660	112,900
Total Income	$ 19,515		$ 23,155		$ 25,815	

(assumes $100,000 starting balance and 5% annual withdrawals)

As you can see from Table 7a, a portfolio of 100% equities would have shrunk from a starting retirement nest egg of $100,000 in October 1973 (the start of the bear market) to under $61,000 in the first year of retirement — a nearly 40% drop in capital. Although the portfolio recovered in later years, the dramatic declines in principal in the initial years and fear of running out of money would have prompted most individuals to cash out. It would have required nerves of steel for a retiree to stick with this investment strategy.

In contrast, and not surprisingly, the 100% fixed-income portfolio fared much better, with a less than 8% decline in capital in the first year. The portfolio provided close to $26,000 in total income and had a balance of about $113,000, a net gain of $13,000, at the end of the five-year period. The balanced portfolio, which was made up of 50% stocks and 50% bonds, although it suffered an initial 25% drop in capital in the first year, yielded $23,155 in total income, and had an end balance of close to $108,000.

When we turn our attention to Table 7b, the bull market scenario, we get the mirror image. The all-equity portfolio delivers the

Table 7b

Retirement Incomes and Bull Markets

Year	100% Equities		50% Equities/50% Bonds		100% Bonds	
	Annual Income	Year-end Balance	Annual Income	Year-end Balance	Annual Income	Year-end Balance
1	$ 5,750	$ 116,000	$ 5,540	$ 111,300	$ 5,295	$ 105,300
2	6,420	125,600	6,065	122,100	5,610	116,000
3	6,315	130,200	6,280	128,800	6,100	124,300
4	7,560	176,600	6,970	151,800	6,275	126,800
5	9,710	215,800	7,975	166,900	6,360	124,900
Total Income	**$ 35,755**		**$ 32,830**		**$ 29,640**	

(assumes $100,000 starting balance and 5% annual withdrawals)

highest income, close to $36,000, over the five-year period and a
capital balance of around $216,000. The fixed-income portfolio,
while it delivers an income of close to $30,000, lags woefully
behind, with an end balance of under $125,000. Again, the bal-
anced portfolio delivers a middle-of-the-road performance, with
income of close to $33,000 and an ending balance of $167,000.

Table 7c

Starting Your Retirement with a Bear Market: A 25-Year Perspective

	100% Equities	50% Equities/ 50% Bonds	100% Bonds
Starting Balance	$ 100,000	$ 100,000	$ 100,000
Ending Balance	389,000	403,000	346,000
Total Withdrawals	271,000	268,000	233,000

(assumes 5% annual withdrawals)

Over a 25-year retirement period, starting with the 1973–74
bear market, the all-equity portfolio would have provided a total
income of $271,000, with a remaining balance of $389,000 (see
Table 7c). The all-bond portfolio would have generated an income
of $233,000 and at the end of the 25-year period would have had a

remaining balance of $346,000. And the balanced portfolio would have provided an income of $268,000 — only marginally less than the all-equity portfolio. Interestingly, the remaining capital for the balanced portfolio at the end of the 25-year period was $403,000, the highest of the three.

Table 7d

Starting Your Retirement with a Bull Market: A 25-Year Perspective

	100% Equities	50% Equities/ 50% Bonds	100% Bonds
Starting Balance	$ 100,000	$ 100,000	$ 100,000
Ending Balance	697,000	557,000	375,000
Total Withdrawals	490,000	386,000	272,000

(assumes 5% annual withdrawals)

Retirees who caught the bull market (see Table 7d) and were invested 100% in equities would have received $490,000 in income over the following 25-year period and would have had an end balance of over $695,000 in their retirement account. The all-bond portfolio would have generated an income of just over $270,000 and would have had an end balance of $375,000. The balanced portfolio would have provided an income of over $385,000, with capital remaining of $557,000.

In hindsight, those who retired at the end of 1974 were lucky. Their retirement happily coincided with the beginning of a bull market. Those who retired a year earlier, in October 1973, were less fortunate — they landed on a particularly savage bear. If the timing is favourable, your retirement will happen simultaneously with a bull market and you will reap the rewards. If it is not, you may encounter a devastating bear and suffer the consequences. Unfortunately, we cannot predict when either will occur.

Bear Markets in Context

Historical data show that since the Second World War, the U.S. stock market, as measured by the S&P 500, has suffered 10 bear markets with declines of 20% or more. During those 10 market declines, stocks dropped an average of 29% over a 15-month period. On a more optimistic note, from the bottom of the last 10 bear markets, stock prices rose on average by close to 140%. In Canada, the TSE 300 has experienced seven bear markets since the mid-1950s, with an average decline of 30%. Although bear markets are part and parcel of any investment equation, they occur fairly infrequently — about once every four and a half years.

The last bear market, which started in the spring of 2000 with the bursting of the technology bubble, was exacerbated by the unparalleled and catastrophic terrorist attack on the World Trade Center in New York City on September 11, 2001. This tragedy reverberated through already volatile markets and left many people not only stunned by the enormity of the assault, but also extremely worried about their exposure to the stock market. The fear (largely unvoiced) of many investors was of a dark period similar to the Great Depression of the 1930s. But was that fear justified?

1929 Revisited

The U.S. stock market crash of 1929 was preceded by a speculative bubble fuelled by factors such as the post–First World War growth boom and high consumer demand. Bear in mind that this was an era when electrical appliances were still a novelty, and every home was eager to have its share of these new labour-saving devices. Moreover, easy-money policies made buying stocks "on margin" highly popular. Requiring only 10% cash down and the remainder on credit, this method of purchase made getting into the market and getting a piece of the action easily accessible to the vast majority. As more and more people purchased stocks, share prices rose, creating more demand and pushing those stock prices ever higher — and further inflating that speculative bubble.

The spring of 1929 heralded a series of stock market declines and recoveries that helped steady investors' nerves through a fairly uneventful summer. But that was just a brief respite before the sell-off began in earnest. On Thursday, October 24, 1929, a record-breaking number of shares — close to 13 million — was traded on the New York Stock Exchange, breaking the previous record of about 4 million shares in March of the previous year. The carnage began in earnest on Tuesday, October 29; by the time the market reached its nadir in mid-1932, the S&P 500 had plummeted by 84.3%.

A Depressing Retirement

The Great Depression, which followed on the heels of the crash of 1929, was unprecedented in its length and the damage it imposed on society as a whole. In 1933, at the depth of the Depression, 16 million people in the United States were unemployed, about one-third of the workforce. The devastating effects were felt not only in the United States but also well outside that country's borders, particularly in Europe, where many countries had not yet recovered from the aftermath of the First World War. Anyone retiring then would have faced monumental challenges, and that's putting it mildly.

Table 7e helps to illustrate what would have happened to the income stream of a retiree who had the misfortune to retire just before the onset of the Great Depression. Starting with a retirement nest egg of $100,000 invested in the stock market, and assuming annual withdrawals of $5,000, the pot would have been empty by 1939, having lasted only 10 years. However, if our retiree had been more savvy and kept yearly withdrawals to a fixed 5%, the pot would still contain $30,000 at the end of the 10-year period. However, the income stream would have varied considerably, ranging from a low of $1,430 to a high of $3,450. (For more on the benefits of percentage withdrawals, see Chapter 14.)

Table 7e

Retirement Incomes and the Great Depression

Year	5% Withdrawal Strategy		$5,000 Withdrawal Strategy	
	Annual Income	Year-end Balance	Annual Income	Year-end Balance
1	$ 3,450	$ 65,600	$ 5,000	$ 64,100
2	2,210	42,000	5,000	38,200
3	1,360	25,800	5,000	19,700
4	1,780	33,800	5,000	22,100
5	1,430	27,200	5,000	13,700
6	1,740	33,000	5,000	12,600
7	2,390	45,400	5,000	13,200
8	2,340	44,500	5,000	8,600
9	1,750	33,200	5,000	1,800
10	1,580	30,100	1,670	0
Total Withdrawals	**$ 20,030**		**$ 46,670**	

(assumes $100,000 starting balance invested in the S&P 500)

Of course, both of these examples, like all illustrations, are more or less set in stone. In reality, people often take actions that either help or hinder their situations, resulting in quite different outcomes.

Could It Happen Again?

Could a catastrophe similar to the Great Depression happen again? While there are no guarantees, it's reassuring to note that many factors have changed since that bleak period. What's more, the Federal Reserve in the United States learned valuable lessons from the crash, which it has since used judiciously. During the market meltdown of October 19, 1987 ("Black Monday"), when the Dow Jones Industrial Average plunged by more than 22% — much more severely than in 1929 — the Federal Reserve moved quickly to lower interest rates and pump liquidity into the system. This expansionary monetary policy helped to contain the potential damage of the crash and reduce the likelihood of greater and broader fallout.

Likewise, the central banks of industrialized nations now adhere to vigilant monetary policies to loosen or tighten the public purse strings in order to adjust to continuous changes in the economic landscape. Markets are also now more mature, and stock exchanges have highly advanced computer systems that can curb the volume of trading to prevent massive sell-offs or buying sprees. And, unlike the way things were back in the 1920s, most industrialized countries now provide social security nets to make sure that all citizens have a modest but secure income base.

But — and there's always a but — that doesn't mean to say that we won't experience prolonged or gut-wrenching market declines (the 2000–2001 bear market being a case in point) or the resulting havoc they can wreak on the portfolios of those who are ill-prepared. Still, there are a few well-tested measures that investors can employ to help protect their retirement savings:

- First of all, retirees should have a well-diversified portfolio that is not only conducive to meeting their income goals but also meshes successfully with their other sources of retirement income, including benefits from the public pension system or a company plan.
- Second, they may want to consider percentage withdrawals based on the current balance of their portfolio, rather than a fixed dollar amount (see Chapter 14).
- Third, because everyone's circumstances and requirements are unique, they should make every effort to get professional advice.

3
Sources of Retirement Income

The Public
Pension System

*A*t some point, if you live long enough — and all studies indicate the majority of us will — you are going to retire from an active working life. Whether you go screaming and resisting or smiling happily is neither here nor there. It's still going to happen. And when your retirement begins, that regular paycheque, which you have relied on throughout your working life, ends.

So how are you going to provide for yourself? Fortunately, in Canada you won't go from something to absolutely nothing. Provided you meet the requirements, you will receive a modest retirement income from our public pension system, which is made up of the Old Age Security program (OAS) and the Canada Pension Plan (CPP) or Quebec Pension Plan (QPP), a parallel program (see Table 8a). In addition, if you receive OAS and have very little other income, you could be eligible for the Guaranteed Income Supplement (GIS) and Allowance.

According to Statistics Canada, about 50% of seniors' income in Canada comes from the public pension system, with the largest share (about 29%) coming from the OAS program and GIS, and 21% from the C/QPP. These programs were set up by federal and provincial laws to provide income security for all seniors and a modest base on which to build for retirement. However, over 25% of seniors in Canada rely exclusively on these programs; without them they would have no other means of support.

Table 8a

OAS and C/QPP Payment Rates*

	Monthly Benefits	
	Average	**Maximum**
OAS**	$ 420.07	$ 442.66
C/QPP	417.23	775.00

*as of December 2001
** Pensioners with an individual net income above $55,309 must repay part or all of the maximum OAS benefit.
Repayment amounts are normally deducted from monthly payments before they are issued. The full OAS pension
is eliminated when a pensioner's net income is $90,195 or above.

Source: HRDC

The Old Age Security Program

The Old Age Security (OAS) program was started in 1952 to make sure that all seniors age 65 and over received a minimum monthly income. To qualify for benefits you must be a Canadian citizen or legal resident and have lived in Canada for at least 10 years after reaching the age of 18. However, you don't need to have worked in Canada to claim OAS, and you can receive this benefit while still working.

How Much Will You Get?
To qualify for the current maximum OAS benefit of just over $5,000 a year (around $440 a month), you need to have lived in Canada for at least 40 years after reaching age 18. But there are a few quirks here. Even if you don't meet this requirement, you may still qualify for the maximum benefit if on July 1, 1977, you were 25 years of age or older, and if you lived in Canada on that date.

You may also qualify if you lived in Canada before that date and had reached 18 years of age or held a valid immigration visa. A definite plus of OAS is that benefits are paid as long as you live and are adjusted to reflect increases in the cost of living. So if inflation rears its ugly head, this portion of your retirement income will keep pace.

The Clawback
All benefits received from OAS are considered taxable income. What's more, retirees with individual after-tax income above the current

limit (for 2001) of $55,309 (based on prior year's income) end up repaying — or having "clawed back" — part of their OAS benefit. For example, if your net income for 2000 was $65,000, your benefit in 2001 would be reduced by 15% of the amount by which your income was above the limit ($65,000 – $55,309 x 15% = $1,453). If you were entitled to the current maximum OAS benefit of about $5,300 a year, this amount would then be reduced to $3,847 ($5,300 – $1,453). Looking at it another way, you lose $150 in OAS benefits for every $1,000 of annual income that is above the current threshold.

If your net income for the prior year was $90,195 or above, your OAS pension would be completely eliminated. Fortunately, or unfortunately, depending how you want to look at it, only about 2% of seniors fall into this category. However, the income threshold, like OAS benefits, is adjusted to reflect any increase in the cost of living as measured by the Consumer Price Index. So, providing this feature remains unchanged, the income threshold will rise in line with the cost of living.

Reducing the Bite

As the income threshold for OAS benefits is determined on an individual basis, a possible way for couples to reduce the clawback is by income-splitting. You want to achieve as equal a distribution of retirement income as possible. One of the best routes to doing this is through the use of spousal registered retirement savings plans (RRSPs), which at retirement allow each spouse to generate income from a separate source. This way you can share a total retirement income of up to around $110,000 and still receive your full OAS benefits. Another option, providing you are both 60 years of age or older, is pension-splitting your C/QPP benefit with your spouse or common-law partner. Unfortunately, single folk can't benefit from either of these options.

If you don't need the extra money and have contributed to an RRSP, you could also delay converting your registered savings plan to retirement income for as long as possible. Currently, the deadline is when you reach 69 years of age. This way you can continue to take full advantage of the plan's tax-free compounding while lowering your total income and hopefully eliminating — or at least minimizing — the OAS clawback.

Other Small but Important Details

If you want to live in Florida, Mexico, or some other warmer climate, go ahead. Provided you have resided in Canada for at least 20 years after the age of 18, retirees who want to live outside Canada can receive benefits no matter which country they choose to reside in. If you have less than the 20 years of residency requirement, but still want to live abroad, you're out of luck. Benefits are paid for only the first six months after departure, and only if you emigrate to a country with a reciprocal agreement with Canada.

So it appears that when you turn 65 years of age, you can just sit back and wait for your pension cheque to arrive in the mail. Wrong! You won't get your OAS pension automatically. You must apply for it, and it's best to do so about six months before you reach 65. If you want, cheques can be automatically deposited into your bank account (Canadian or American) or mailed to your home address. Payments are normally received during the last three business days of each month. For more information on the OAS program, call 1-800-277-9914; for an application form, call 1-877-454-4051.

The Guaranteed Income Supplement and Allowance

The Guaranteed Income Supplement (GIS) was introduced in 1967 to provide additional income, beyond the OAS pension, to low-income seniors living in Canada. To be eligible for this tax-free supplement, you must receive an OAS pension and have little or no other income. This means that if you are a single person, you must have an annual income under the current limit, which is about $12,600. For couples, if you and your partner both receive OAS benefits, your combined annual income from all sources must be less than around $16,400 to qualify.

The average GIS benefit is currently about $360 a month for a single person, $200 for the partner of a pensioner, and $335 for the partner of a non-pensioner. If you're thinking of retiring outside Canada, it's important to note that you will receive the benefit for a maximum of only six months from the date of departure. For more information on the GIS, call 1-800-277-9914.

The Allowance (formerly the Spouse's Pension Allowance) is payable between 60 and 64 years of age, and was designed to help widowed persons and couples living on just one OAS pension. To qualify for this benefit, you must be a Canadian citizen or a legal resident and have resided in Canada for at least 10 years after reaching the age of 18. At the end of 2001, the maximum monthly amount payable was about $785 (regular) and $865 (widowed), but the average payout for the same period was considerably less, at $281 (regular) and $461 (widowed). To qualify, your yearly income must fall below a certain amount, and the further your income is under this amount, the more you will receive, up to the maximum limit. To find out if you are eligible for this tax-free benefit, call 1-800-277-9914.

The Canada Pension Plan and Quebec Pension Plan

The Canada and Quebec pension plans (CPP and QPP) were established in 1966 to provide income security for a contributor and his or her family upon retirement, disability, or death. The CPP operates in nine provinces and the territories, while the QPP, a parallel plan, operates in Quebec. Both plans are compulsory, contributory, public pension plans covering Canadian workers age 18 to 70 who have annual earned incomes of between $3,500 and the current average industrial wage of $38,300. When you retire, benefits from the plan could replace up to a maximum of 25% of your pre-retirement income, based on the average wage. If you were retiring today, that would translate into an annual benefit of about $9,500. Currently about 5 million Canadians receive C/QPP benefits.

One of the key advantages of this plan is its availability to all workers across Canada. As long as you earn $3,500 (the current minimum) or more annually, your monthly contribution will be deducted at source. The plan, unlike most company pension plans, has no vesting requirements and restrictions ("vesting" simply means when you are eligible for 100% of the accumulated contributions). Social Security in the United States requires that you complete 40 calendar quarters of employment over a lifetime to be eligible for benefits, but CPP requires only one month. In addition, no matter how long you work or how many job changes you make, your contributions are fully transferable from company to company.

Unlike the OAS program, which is funded out of federal general tax revenues, the CPP and QPP are funded by the combined (and equal) contributions of employees and employers and by the returns on invested monies not required to pay current benefits. So if you have never paid into either of these plans, don't expect to take anything out of them. However, this may be a moot point for pessimists who regard the viability of the CPP fund as unsustainable.

Most experts would agree that the fund has been on somewhat shaky ground, given the demographic pressures of an aging society, a low birth rate, and a rapidly shifting economy. But the federal and provincial governments have introduced new measures to ensure its financial soundness and viability for Canadians in the future. These include raising the combined employee/employer contribution rate from the current 7.8% to 9.9% by 2003, seeking higher returns by investing in a diversified portfolio of securities (previous investments were limited to non-negotiable provincial bonds, with their concomitant lower returns), and decreasing some benefits. (The future of our pension plans is discussed in more detail in Chapter 2.)

When Can You Apply?

Your CPP pension normally begins the month after your 65th birthday — which is considered the normal retirement age — whether or not you are still working. But you can take it as early as age 60 (with reduced benefits), provided you have more or less stopped working, and as late as age 70 (with increased benefits).

How Much Will You Get?

The amount you receive will depend on how much and for how long you contributed to the plan. Monthly pension benefits in 2001 ranged anywhere from $2, to the average payment of around $415, up to the maximum of about $775. Many people assume that, because they have been working for what seems like most of their lives, they will receive the maximum benefit. Maybe — but then again, maybe not! In order to be eligible for the maximum payment, you would not only need to have worked for 40 years, but also to have paid the maximum CPP contribution each and every year.

On a more positive note, payment rates are adjusted upwards every January to reflect increases in the rate of inflation. So, if we are faced with double-digit inflation reminiscent of what we experienced in the 1980s, the C/QPP portion of your retirement income (provided this feature is not tampered with) will be well protected.

For a better fix on how much you will receive, you should take a close look at your annual Statement of Contributions from the federal government. This statement gives an estimate of your monthly retirement pension at age 65. Bear in mind that this estimated amount is based on the assumption that you will continue to work until age 65. If you decide to retire earlier, the amount you will receive may be less. If you have not received a statement and you have made at least one contribution to the CPP, call the federal government's Human Resources Development Canada (HRDC) at 1-800-277-9914. In Quebec, check your telephone directory for the nearest office of the Régie des rentes du Quebec for information on the QPP.

When Should You Start Collecting Your Pension?

If you opt for an early retirement, your pension will be reduced by 0.5% a month for each month you receive the benefit before age 65. This means that if you were eligible for the maximum benefit of $775 and you decided to retire at age 60, your payments would be reduced by 30%, to $542. On the other hand, if you postponed retirement to age 70, your payments would increase by 30%, to

$1,007. (However, if you wait to apply until after you have reached age 70, you could lose some benefits.)

The decision on when to start collecting your pension is purely a personal one. Factors to consider include your health and the possible tax implications. If you are in good health and your family members typically live well into their 80s or 90s, you might want to delay receiving your benefits until later to receive the extra amount. However, if you take the benefit at the normal retirement age of 65 years, even though you receive more money every month, it will take you about 10 years to catch up to the total benefits paid out to someone who started collecting at 60.

Also, if you need the money to meet monthly expenses or are in poor health, it would undoubtedly make more sense to start receiving your pension benefits sooner rather than later. Getting some input from a professional, such as your financial advisor or accountant, could help you clarify which route is best for you, based on your personal circumstances.

Other Benefits

The CPP is not restricted to simply providing contributors with retirement income; it also provides built-in life and disability insurance. If you take a look at your Statement of Contributions, you will see that it gives an estimate of the monthly payment you would receive if you became disabled and, in the event of your death, what benefit would be paid to your survivors. What's more, there is also a one-time death benefit of up to $2,500 that goes to the surviving spouse, or whoever is responsible for funeral expenses. You should be aware that contributions made by either spouse may be divided equally in the event of divorce or separation. If you qualify for this option, both partners become eligible for a retirement pension and possibly other CPP benefits.

Reducing the Tax Bite

Because all benefits are considered taxable income, it's important to think about strategies that will allow you to keep more of your money. The best advice is to get help from a qualified financial or tax professional. But here's one approach you may want to consider: on retirement, if one spouse is receiving more income than the other, and you are both 60 years of age or more, you can opt to pension-split. Sharing your pension could help reduce the tax bite by moving the higher income earner into a lower tax bracket.

Another possible option is to delay receiving benefits until your income from other sources is lower. This could also put you in a lower tax bracket and may decrease the amount of OAS that is clawed back.

To get more information on splitting C/QPP benefits or for copies of the appropriate forms, call 1-877-454-4051.

Other Important Points

- Under the present system, guaranteed monthly benefits are paid out for as long as you live, with reduced payments going to any eligible beneficiaries. This means that a person who lives to a very old age will get a large total benefit under the current program, but one who dies earlier could end up with far less. Either way, even though you may have contributed the maximum for 40 years, there is no residual lump sum for your estate. This remains a bone of contention for many people.
- C/QPP benefits must be applied for, and it's best to do so about six months before you want to start receiving payment. If you want, cheques can be automatically deposited into your bank account (Canadian or American), or can be mailed to your home address. You should expect to receive your payment during the last three business days of each month. For more information on the CPP, call 1-800-277-9914; for an application form, call

1-877-454-4051. For information on the QPP, contact the nearest office of the Régie des rentes du Quebec.

- If living on the current maximum OAS and C/QPP combined benefits (about $2,400 a month for a couple and $1,200 if you're single) is going to be sufficient for your retirement needs, great! But remember, you'll receive these amounts only at age 65, *and* only if you qualify for the maximum benefits. If relying solely on these benefits will mean a dramatic and unwanted drop in your standard of living, you had better take some remedial action. Otherwise, brace yourself for what could be some very tough years ahead.

Company Pension Plans

9

Company pension plans, often called registered pension plans (RPPs), are essentially professionally managed investment pools offered by employers to help fund their employees' retirements. While some plans are funded by the employer (non-contributory plans), others are paid for solely by the employee or by both employee and employer (contributory plans). Between 1981 and 1997, the proportion of seniors' income coming from RPPs increased significantly, rising from 12% to 21%. So, as a source of income in retirement, these plans are playing an increasingly important role for many Canadians. A recent Statistics Canada Survey of Financial Security found that 47% of Canadian families had assets in company pension plans, with the median value of those assets at just under $50,000 — meaning that half of the family units had assets above this level and half were below. In total, the assets in these plans are estimated at $604 billion.

The four main types of pension plans that most companies offer are defined benefit (DB), defined contribution (DC), group registered retirement savings plans (RRSPs), and deferred profit-sharing plans (DPSPs).

Defined Benefit Plans

Defined benefit plans are "traditional" pension plans, in that they are generally fully paid for by the employer and guarantee a monthly pension cheque for a specific amount for life. However, like many traditions, this one is beginning to show signs of a decline in popularity. Although they are still the most common pension plans in large, well-established corporations and government, newer companies are more inclined to favour DC plans, which are much more suitable to today's more mobile workforce.

The biggest benefit of a DB plan is its guarantee of a monthly pension cheque for a specific amount for life. In addition, the employer is responsible for making all the contributions to the plan so that there is adequate money available to pay employees on retirement. For many Canadians, a defined benefit plan will be their most valuable asset; in retirement it could replace up to as much as 70% of their pre-retirement income.

How Much Will You Get?

The amount you receive in retirement from a defined benefit plan is typically based on a number of factors. These include your years of service, your average salary over your entire career or an average of the last five or six years' earnings (normally the highest annual salaries of an employee's career), and a percentage multiplier.

You can get a good ballpark figure of how much you will receive if you know the benefit factor for your plan. Let's say you have worked for the company for 25 years, the average income for your best five working years is $40,000, and your plan pays 1.25% (the benefit factor). You're looking at a retirement income of about $12,500 a year (25 x $40,000 x 1.25%).

For other plans, the size of your pension could be determined by your years of service and your final salary. With a 1.25% benefit factor, a 20-year career will provide a pension that will replace about 25% of pre-retirement income (20 x 1.25%). With the same benefit factor, a 40-year career will provide a pension that will replace about 50% of pre-retirement income. Benefit factors typically range between 1% and 1.5%, although a few plans, such as those offered by federal and provincial governments, may go as high as 2%.

Vesting Requirements

If you frequently change jobs, a common occurrence in today's working world, you may lose your benefits if you have not been with the company long enough. Vesting (when you are eligible for 100% of the accumulated contributions) generally occurs — in most provinces — two years after joining the plan. If you have met the vesting requirements and decide to pursue a job opportunity elsewhere, you can leave your pension "as is" and collect the estimated benefits when you retire.

Other options include transferring the accumulated amount to your new employer or to a locked-in RRSP, also called a locked-in retirement account (LIRA) in some provinces. A locked-in account is essentially the same as a personal RRSP, except that you can't make any further contributions and there are restrictions on withdrawals.

Advantages and Disadvantages of DBS

The major benefit of a DB plan is, of course, that you will receive a guaranteed pension income of a specific amount for as long as you live. For many people, this promise of future income will be their most valuable asset. To get some understanding of its worth, for every $10,000 a year in guaranteed retirement income received from the plan, you would need to have accumulated anywhere between $100,000 and $125,000 in retirement savings to generate the same income. Another major plus of defined benefit plans is the fact that the employers take all the investment risk. Regardless of how the stock market performs, they are obliged to pay employees a certain pension. In other words, it is the company's responsibility to find the money to fulfil its promise to provide a specific pension package. Such was the predicament of the Church of England in late 2001, when it announced it would need to find another £12 million ($27.7 million) a year to shore up its pension fund. In addition, some defined benefit pensions, unlike defined contribution and group RRSP pensions, may be fully or partially indexed to inflation.

The biggest disadvantage is that when you die there is no

remaining lump sum for your survivors or estate. Of course, a surviving spouse or other eligible dependants would continue to receive monthly cheques, but they would typically be for only about 60% of the original pension. Other drawbacks for the plan holder might include lack of options. In an emergency, or if you simply need some extra cash in retirement, you're out of luck. You will continue to receive your regular monthly cheque, but cannot withdraw any additional amounts.

It is possible that your pension may be integrated with your C/QPP benefits. This is something you should definitely check up on. You don't want to base your retirement income projections on the assumption that you will be receiving a company pension *plus* C/QPP, and then find out at retirement that your supposition was wrong.

Also, some pensions impose a cap on the number of years on which you can earn benefits. Even if you work to age 65, you might not receive a higher pension. There is also a risk that the company may experience tough times and initiate cutbacks in benefit payments at some time in the future.

And of course, as with all other company pension plans, membership in a defined benefit plan will reduce the annual amount that you are eligible to contribute to an individual RRSP.

Defined Contribution Plans

Defined contribution (DC) plans, also known as "money purchase" plans, are becoming the pension vehicle of choice for many employers. With this type of plan, you and your employer contribute a certain amount every year in your name, up to a set limit. In some plans, to encourage a higher savings rate, the company will match their employees' contributions. As companies move away from defined benefit plans, DC plans have become the popular choice for employers.

How Much Will You Get?

Unlike defined benefit plans, defined contribution plans don't guarantee a specific retirement income for life. Instead, your retirement income will depend on numerous factors. These include the total dollar amount contributed to the plan, your investment strategy, your choice of investments — which will depend on the options offered by the plan — and the performance of those investments. You will not know the actual dollar value of your plan until the day you retire. You can use various computer programs to give you a ballpark figure, but that's all it will be. Your investments may do worse (or better) than the software assumes.

Vesting Requirements

Although vesting for some DC plans takes about two years after joining, most companies allow vesting immediately. When it comes to portability, you usually have the same choices as with DBs: leave "as is" until retirement, transfer to a new employer, or open a locked-in retirement account.

Advantages and Disadvantages of DCs

One of the advantages for today's more mobile employees is that DC plans are easier to transfer than DB plans. They also often allow senior employees to contribute more; if your company offers this option, you should definitely take full advantage of it. On retirement, a defined contribution plan can be converted to an annuity, which will provide a regular stream of retirement income. Other options include a life income fund (LIF) or a locked-in retirement income fund (LRIF). You can read more on these retirement income alternatives in chapters 12 and 13.

On the down side, unlike in the defined benefit plan, the investment risk and the responsibility for providing future retirement income fall squarely on the shoulders of the employee (the employee is under no obligation to pay a specific pension). What's more, the final dollar amount of the pension plan will not be known until the date of retirement. As mentioned earlier, that will depend on total contributions, investment choices, and the return on the invested money. Also, as DC plans are rarely indexed to inflation, you are going to have to accumulate substantially more in order to compensate.

Group Registered Retirement Savings Plans

Group RRSPs are generally the retirement vehicle of choice for smaller companies. A group RRSP is simply an informal pooling of individual retirement plans that a company offers as a benefit to its employees. The plans are typically managed by financial institutions, mutual fund companies, and investment planning firms. Generally speaking, the employees are the sole contributors, while their employer covers the administrative costs. With this type of plan, the employees decide how much they will contribute (up to regular RRSP limits) and the amount is automatically deducted from their paycheques. In order to increase participation, some innovative companies have been known to raise salaries on condition that a certain amount be contributed to the plan.

How Much Will You Get?
Similarly to DC plans, group RRSPs don't guarantee a specific amount at retirement. The amount you accumulate will depend on various factors, including number of contributing years, the dollar amount you have contributed, your choice of investments, and the performance of those investments.

Vesting Requirements
Most companies with group RRSPs allow their employees to join the plan after they have been with them for a year or less. If you leave the company after that time, you can transfer your contributions to your new employer.

Advantages and Disadvantages of Group RRSPs
With an average vesting requirement of one year or less, group RRSPs are especially portable company pension plans. On retire-

ment, you also have the option — not available with DBs and DCs — of taking a lump-sum cash payment. However, unless it is a fairly small amount, the cash payment probably wouldn't be a good choice, as it would be counted as taxable income. If you want to delay giving your money to the taxman for as long as possible, and ensure some additional retirement income, you can roll your group RRSP holdings into a RRIF or buy an annuity. (For more on RRIFs, see Chapter 11; for annuities, see Chapter 13.)

One of the biggest shortcomings of RRSPs is that they are not compulsory. It is up to the employees to determine if they will participate. Many don't, leaving them particularly vulnerable when retirement rolls around. Another possible drawback is the investment options, as the plans that some companies provide don't offer much in the way of choice. And because these plans do not provide an "indexed to inflation" feature, you are going to have to contribute more in order to compensate.

Deferred Profit-Sharing Plans

If you work for a company that has a deferred profit-sharing plan (DPSP), your employer makes contributions on your behalf that are based on the company's profits. The dollar amount of the contribution will depend on your salary and the length of time you have been employed by the company. Typically, an employer will contribute at least 1% of participating employees' annual salaries each year that the company makes a profit. If the company doesn't make a profit in a year, they don't have to make any contributions.

Money in a DPSP is allowed to grow tax-free, and on retirement, you can take the cash or use your DPSP proceeds to buy an annuity or transfer them to a registered plan. You would, of course, have to pay income tax on any cash withdrawals, so get some professional advice before deciding on this course of action. Of course, the success of DPSPs, as for stock options, relies completely on the initiating company. Many workers have found out the hard way the dangers of overloading on company stock. The recent Enron Corporation debacle resulted in some workers facing losses on their retirement savings of as much as US$800,000 when the company's stock fell from around US$90.00 in the summer of 2000 to US$0.36 by the beginning of 2002.

Getting Answers

If you are unsure about any aspect of your company's pension plan, you should set up a meeting with the person who is responsible within your company, usually someone in the human resources department. A list of questions you may want to ask is included in Appendix A.

Personal Savings

The amount of personal savings accumulated during their working years will, for most people, have a decided impact on their retirement lifestyle. In 1998 around 17% of all the income of seniors came from their personal savings. Your savings — whether they are in individual RRSPs, real estate, or gold bars or sitting in a bank account — can, if sufficient, provide you with the additional funds to indulge in your retirement dreams. If they are inadequate, depending on your other sources of retirement income, you could see a significant, abrupt, and unintended drop in your standard of living.

Baby boomers may be especially vulnerable; unlike their parents' generation, they expect retirement lifestyle to resemble that of their relatively affluent working years. But unless they have taken the necessary steps to ensure that they will have sufficient funds in retirement to sustain that standard of living, many baby boomers will be forced to accept a decidedly more frugal lifestyle. What's more, it might deteriorate further over the course of what could be 30 years of retirement. Not a pleasant scenario, and one that can be avoided — or at the very least, mitigated — by some additional income to rely on. While there are many ways to accumulate extra retirement income, one of the easiest is through a registered retirement savings plan.

Registered Retirement Savings Plans

A registered retirement savings plan (RRSP) is a tax shelter, provided under the Income Tax Act, that gives individuals who file a tax return in Canada and have eligible earned income the opportunity to save money for their retirement. According to the recent *Survey of Financial Security* released by Statistics Canada, more than half of all Canadian families now hold RRSPs. That's a sharp increase from 1984, when only 28% put their money into these plans.

While this news is encouraging, it doesn't mean that we can all heave a collective sigh of relief. The amounts being contributed to RRSPs slowed considerably from 1997 to 1999, rising by only about 1% during that period. This is in sharp contrast to biennial increases of 20% to 28% since 1991. As you might expect, the older Canadians get, the more they are likely to have in their RRSPs. But what you might not expect is, to put it bluntly, the relatively small amounts Canadians are accumulating. Either they have exceedingly generous company pension plans or money stashed away in the Caymans, or they are counting on winning the lottery, or they are planning a short retirement. Otherwise, one can only assume that they are going to adopt a rather thrifty retirement lifestyle. For the 45-to-54 age group in Statistics Canada's report, the *median* value of RRSPs was only $30,000. This means that half the families surveyed had less than that amount. In the 55-to-64 age group, the median value was not much better, at $50,000. If this group retired today, assuming annual withdrawals of no more than 5%, their savings would generate roughly $210 a month in income.

An important feature of RRSPs is that you can keep contributing until the end of the year in which you reach 69 (which is probably just as well, given their current dollar values). So even if you've been procrastinating about saving for your retirement, or haven't been contributing, you have a wide window of opportunity. The contribution limit for RRSPs is 18% of your previous year's earned income, to a maximum of $13,500, minus any pension plan adjustments such as contributions to a DC plan. In other words, if you earned $40,000 in the previous year, you would be able to contribute up to your 18% limit of $7,200, minus your company pension plan contribution. If you were not a member of any pension plan, you would be able to contribute the full $7,200. The 18% limit remains in effect until 2003. After that date, the maximum contribution limits are $14,500 for 2004 and $15,500 for the 2005 tax year. After that, the maximum contribution will be indexed to inflation.

RRSPs are not complicated; you can set one up through a financial advisor, bank, mutual fund company, or discount brokerage. When it comes to the investments to hold in your plan, there is a wide range to choose from, including all categories of mutual funds and individual bonds and stocks.

Spousal RRSPs

If you are married and the higher income earner, you may want to consider investing all or a portion of your maximum allowable contribution in a spousal RRSP. These contributions can be deducted from your taxable income, but the plan belongs to your spouse. The amount contributed will not affect his or her yearly limit. For example, if your limit is $13,500 and your partner's is $6,500, you could put $3,500 into a plan in your spouse's name. That way, you each end up with a $10,000 contribution.

If the total amount in your partner's RRSP is well below yours, you should consider contributing the entire $13,500 to a spousal plan in his or her name. Contributing to a spousal RRSP allows you to split income more effectively in retirement, which could mean that you get to keep more, or all, of your OAS benefit. It could also save you tax dollars by moving you into a lower tax bracket in retirement.

How Much Will You Get?

Similarly to DC plans and group RRSPs, individual RRSPs don't guarantee a specific amount at retirement. The amount accumulated will depend on various factors, including the total number of contributing years, the dollar amount you have contributed, your choice of investments, and the performance of those investments. In other words, the sooner you start, the more you contribute, and the higher the rate of return on your investments, the larger your retirement nest egg.

Advantages and Disadvantage of RRSPs

The two main benefits of investing in this type of plan are tax reduction and tax-free compounding. Depending on your tax bracket, every $1,000 contributed will save you about $250 to $500 in taxes for the year that you make the contribution. In other words, the higher your income, the more tax you will save. As for tax-free compounding, it means that all the money in your RRSP, including all distributions and capital gains, is not subject to taxation. This makes a huge difference in the amount of money you'll be able to accumulate for retirement. Taxes are paid only when you withdraw the money.

Another advantage is that, at termination, RRSPs give you plenty of options. You can withdraw all or a portion of the plan's proceeds and pay the required taxes. As the amount would be included in your income for the year of withdrawal and taxed at your marginal tax rate, this might not be the best course of action to take — unless, of course, it is a relatively small amount. Other options include transferring the plan's proceeds or the investments it holds to a registered retirement income fund (RRIF) or using them to purchase an annuity. You can also, of course, do any combination of the three. (For more on RRIFs, see Chapter 11; for annuities, see Chapter 13.)

The biggest drawback to this type of plan — and it's really more of an annoying inconvenience — is the amount of time it may take to move from one administrator to another. If, for example, you have your RRSP set up with one bank or company and you wish to switch to another, it could take several weeks before the transaction is complete. If you wish to make a trade while your plan is in transit, you're out of luck.

Non-Registered Investments

Some people are in the fortunate position of having many nest eggs stashed away for retirement. In addition to a company pension plan and an RRSP, they may also have some non-registered investments. These are savings and investments that are not tax-sheltered, and might include money held in a savings account, GICs, mutual funds, stocks, or bonds.

Unlike registered income funds, from which you must withdraw a certain percentage every year, non-registered investments provide much more flexibility for individuals. If they need some extra money at retirement, they can withdraw as much or as little as they want from their bank account or cash in a few stocks. This additional source of income is tax-free, because only the interest or dividend income and capital gains from the investments held are subject to tax. The withdrawn funds will therefore not affect OAS benefits or move the retiree into a higher tax bracket.

Real Estate

For many people, their home will represent the largest part of their total wealth, and as such will be a potential source of retirement income. However, don't automatically assume you will be one of them. Thirty-five percent of homeowners still have a mortgage to pay off when they retire!

If you plan to be mortgage-free when you stop working, one popular option is to downsize — to move from a larger home to a smaller one — and use the realized capital gain to provide additional retirement income. The catch here is, of course, that you cannot predict whether the real estate market will be booming or in a slump. You may get a buyer immediately or have the house on the market for an extended period. Also, unlike the previous generation, baby boomers have not had the impetus of inflation to boost house prices, so you may get much less for your home than anticipated. You may also end up paying more for your new, downsized home than you had expected, leaving you with a smaller retirement income pool. To avoid any unpleasant surprises, it's always best to be conservative in your projections.

Some retirees, providing their home is suitable, elect to share their accommodation with other family members. The family in turn agree to take responsibility for some or all of the ongoing household expenses, such as taxes and maintenance costs. The benefits to the retiree include retention of home ownership, additional disposable income, companionship, and security — not to mention someone else to shovel the snow and mow the lawn! For many elderly retirees, these advantages may well outweigh the potential loss of independence and privacy.

Reverse Mortgages

If you need the additional income, but the mere thought of selling or sharing your home drives your blood pressure to new heights, there is another route to consider. One way to get equity out of your home, *and* continue to live in it, is through a reverse mortgage. This is similar to a conventional mortgage, but in reverse — hence the name. Instead of you paying off a mortgage to a financial institution, the financial institution pays you for the equity it now holds in your home.

A reverse mortgage allows you to convert a portion of your home's value into cash. The money, which is generally between 10% and 40% of the value of your home, can be taken as a lump-sum cash payment, as monthly income, or in a combination. Many retirees use the proceeds of a reverse mortgage to travel, buy a second home in a warmer climate, give financial aid to their children, or simply supplement their income. For couples, a reverse mortgage could also be used to offset a reduction in income when one partner dies.

The amount you will receive depends on various factors, including your age and the location and value of your property. Generally speaking, the older you are, the higher the percentage you will get. Most reverse mortgages allow several repayment options, including no repayments as long as you live in your home; repaying the annual interest only or the entire amount within a specified number of years; or full repayment when the home is sold. To qualify for a reverse mortgage, you must be 62 or older and must own (or nearly own) your home, and there can be no tax liens against it. When you die and your property is sold, the proceeds are used to pay off the mortgage.

While a reverse mortgage may sound like the answer to your retirement income needs, proceed thoughtfully. After having been mortgage-free, it may be difficult for you to go back to having someone else own a piece of your home. Also, a reverse mortgage does not free you from paying the taxes, putting on a new roof, or any of the other costs associated with ownership. Before proceeding, it's sensible to get advice from a qualified professional, such as an accountant or financial advisor who specializes in retirement issues.

A Final Word

Securing your retirement lifestyle, whether it be spending part of the year in warmer climates, living year-round at the cottage, or indulging in an expensive hobby, takes many attributes, including commitment, knowledge, effort, and — most important of all — planning. It would be reasonable to say that many people spend more time organizing their annual vacation than they do their retirement. Those people simply put the retirement issue in their "pending" file. The trouble is, they leave it there!

4

*Funding
Your Retirement*

Registered Retirement
Income Funds

11

What do you do with your retirement savings once you retire? If you have a registered retirement savings plan (RRSP) or an eligible company pension plan (one that is not locked in), you basically have three options. You can cash out a portion or all of your money. But unless you're in a lower tax bracket and it's quite a small amount, this course of action is not recommended, as the tax consequences could be quite severe.

Other options are to use your RRSP funds to purchase an annuity (see Chapter 13) or to transfer the funds to a registered retirement income fund (RRIF). Of course, you can also use any combination of the above choices; this is not an either/or situation. For instance, you could take a taxable cash payment to pay for that cruise you had always promised yourself, purchase an annuity that would provide income to cover your living expenses, and transfer the remaining funds tax-free to a RRIF.

What Is a RRIF?

A RRIF is simply a fund set up with the proceeds from an RRSP or an eligible company pension to provide income during retirement. RRIFs are a popular retirement income vehicle because they allow you to hold the same type of investments that you had in your registered retirement plan. With a regular RRIF, you can hold mutual funds, guaranteed investment certificates (GICs), and Canada Savings

Bonds. If you also want to hold individual stocks and bonds, you can open, for a small annual administrative fee, a self-directed RRIF.

The big difference between RRSPs and RRIFs is that with an RRIF you can no longer contribute money, but must instead start withdrawing your savings. But, as with an RRSP, all interest income and capital gains generated by the investments contained within a RRIF can still continue to grow tax-free. This is an important benefit, made more so by the possibility of having to fund 20 or 30 years of retirement. Not only does it allow you to maximize your income potential, but it also ensures that taxes are paid only on the amounts withdrawn. Even then, many plan-holders find that the tax rate on their RRIF withdrawals is much lower, because their income in retirement is not as high as when they were employed.

When Can You Open a RRIF?

You may open a RRIF at any time, but the deadline is December 31 of the year in which you turn 69 years old. As some company pension plans have restrictions on when you can withdraw your money, you should check with your employer well ahead of time to find out the details. (See Appendix A for more questions to ask about your company pension plan.) Transferring the proceeds of your RRSP or company plan to a RRIF is quite simple. The administrator of your plan will help you arrange for a *direct transfer* to your RRIF custodian, often a bank or mutual fund company. This direct transfer is essential. It ensures that you won't be liable for any taxes on the plan's proceeds, as you would be if you received a cheque in your name.

You should also give yourself plenty of time to review your retirement income needs and investment options. In other words, don't leave these important decisions until the last minute. In fact, five to 10 years before retirement is a good time to review your RRSP or company pension plan holdings. You may want to start gradually reallocating your assets with a view to future retirement income.

Unless you are a knowledgeable and experienced investor, you, like most people, will benefit from some professional advice and help.

How Much Can You Withdraw?

Once you open a RRIF, you must take out at least the minimum withdrawal amount every year, starting the year after you open the account. You also must start withdrawals no later than the end of the year in which you turn 70. Your minimum annual withdrawal is determined by the amount of money in your plan at the beginning of that year, as well as your age. Table 11a shows the different percentages that must be withdrawn on a yearly basis as stipulated by the Canada Customs and Revenue Agency (CCRA). As you can see, the withdrawal percentage increases annually to a maximum of 20% a year at age 94 and older.

As the table shows, there are different withdrawal rules if you bought your RRIF prior to 1993. For ages 71 through 77, the required minimum annual withdrawal is less, resulting in smaller payments. At 71, for example, with a balance at the beginning of the year of $100,000 in your plan, the minimum annual withdrawal of 5.26% would provide a taxable income of $5,260 for that year. In contrast, RRIFs purchased in 1993 or after would provide $7,380. However, at age 78 the withdrawal rates merge and are identical from that point on.

As there are no stipulations about the timing of annual withdrawals, you can spread them over, say, six or 12 equal payments, whatever suits you best. Or, if you prefer, you can take your withdrawal as one lump sum. To maximize tax-deferred growth, you can also choose to delay taking the withdrawal until year-end. This would allow your investments to grow tax-free for the entire 12-month period. To calculate your minimum withdrawal, simply refer to Table 11a, find your age and the corresponding percentage according to when you purchased your plan, and multiply that by the value of your RRIF at the beginning of the year.

Table 11a

Minimum RRIF Withdrawal Rates

Your Age	RRIFs Purchased Before 1993	RRIFS Purchased in 1993 or Later
69	4.76 %	4.76 %
70	5.00	5.00
71	5.26	7.38
72	5.56	7.48
73	5.88	7.59
74	6.25	7.71
75	6.67	7.85
76	7.14	7.99
77	7.69	8.15
78	8.33	8.33
79	8.53	8.53
80	8.75	8.75
81	8.99	8.99
82	9.27	9.27
83	9.58	9.58
84	9.93	9.93
85	10.33	10.33
86	10.79	10.79
87	11.33	11.33
88	11.96	11.96
89	12.71	12.71
90	13.62	13.62
91	14.73	14.73
92	16.12	16.12
93	17.92	17.92
94 and older	20.00	20.00

Early Retirement

If you open a RRIF before the age of 69, you can calculate your minimum annual withdrawal by using a simple formula. Take the value of your RRIF at the beginning of the year in which you wish to start withdrawals and divide it by 90 minus your age. Let's say you want to start withdrawals at 60 years of age and have $300,000 in your RRIF at the beginning of the year. The minimum amount you would have to withdraw is $10,000 ($300,000 ÷ 30). The same formula would apply for each successive year until the required withdrawal rates kicked in.

Delaying the Tax Bite

If you are married, and your RRIF will not be your primary source of income, you have the option of tying the withdrawals to your spouse's age. As the minimum withdrawal percentage increases as you get older, it is usually a good idea to use a younger spouse's age to start with. This allows you to delay paying income tax on the bulk of your retirement savings as long as possible, and allows maximum growth of your investments on a tax-deferred basis. If you decide to choose this option, you must do so when you open your RRIF. Once committed, you cannot reverse the decision.

Withholding Tax

While you are allowed to withdraw more than the annual minimum from your RRIF, there is an up-front cost involved. Table 11b shows the amount of tax that is withheld at source on any amounts that exceed the minimum withdrawal limits stipulated by the CCRA. This withholding tax is essentially an estimated prepayment of taxes that may actually be owed. This means that if you lived in any

Table 11b

Withholding Taxes on RRIF Withdrawals

Amount of Withdrawal in Excess of Minimum Amount	All Provinces Except Quebec	Quebec
Up to $ 5,000	10 %	24 %
$ 5,001 to $ 15,000	20	32
Over $ 15,000	30	37

province except Quebec, and withdrew an extra $10,000 from your RRIF (over and above the minimum withdrawal for the year), the 20% withholding tax would reduce the amount received to $8,000. In Quebec, with its higher penalty of 32%, an extra $10,000 lump-sum withdrawal would be reduced to $6,800.

Before dipping into your retirement savings, you should bear in mind that any extra withdrawals will eat into your capital and could seriously diminish your future stream of income. Another point to consider is the tax consequences. Will that extra withdrawal put you in a higher tax bracket? And will it have a negative impact on your OAS benefit? Currently, retirees with individual after-tax incomes above $55,309 (based on the previous year's income) end up repaying — having "clawed back" — part of their OAS benefit. Other tax credits could also be affected.

Advantages and Disadvantages

One of the key benefits of RRIFs is that they are designed, through their minimum withdrawals, so that you will receive a steady stream of income throughout your retirement and will never run out of money. The gradual increase in the percentage of withdrawals also provides built-in protection against inflation. Another big advantage is that the investments held within the plan continue to grow tax-free. Outside a registered plan, 50% of all capital gains are subject to tax, and investments that provide interest income — which many retirees favour — receive no tax breaks whatsoever.

RRIFs also allow you to continue to diversify your investments according to your retirement income needs and risk tolerance, and you are free to change your investment mix at any time. For example, you could take advantage of a hike in interest rates by moving some money into higher-yielding investments. Or, if you felt that interest rates were attractively high, you could decide to cash in all or a portion of your RRIF and purchase an annuity.

Although the withdrawal regulations have their benefits, they also, like many things in life, have a vulnerable spot. Under RRIF rules, you *have* to take a minimum amount of money out of your plan every year, regardless of market conditions. This withdrawing of money on a regular basis is the antithesis of dollar-cost averaging. With dollar-cost averaging, you are *contributing* on a regular basis, thereby taking advantage of market highs and lows and averaging out the dollar cost of your investments. You can cushion the effects of a market decline on your overall portfolio by continuing to buy when prices are near or at the bottom. When the market takes off, these investments will show a profit.

Unfortunately, you get the exact opposite effect with a RRIF. Continuing to withdraw on a regular basis during market declines forces you into the position of selling your investments at a loss. In a prolonged market downturn, this could have a significant impact on the total dollar value of your holdings and could seriously affect your future income potential. This would be especially true if a bear market occurred at or near the beginning of your retirement. The frightening thing is that this is something you have absolutely no control over. You may be lucky or you may not. That's why it's crucial to ensure that you have the right mix of investments in your RRIF. Because, let's face it, a continued downward slide in the total dollar value of what is perhaps a significant source of one's retirement income would be a very scary prospect for most retirees. (Refer back to Chapter 7 for the possible impact of a bull or bear market on retirement incomes.)

Dealing with Fluctuating Income Streams

One plus of being in the workforce is that you receive a regular paycheque. It doesn't matter whether markets are bearish or bullish or if interest rates are trending up or down. Market movements — positive or negative — will have no direct impact on your income. But in retirement it's a different ball game. Depending on the investments held in your RRIF, those same market movements could have either ominous or favourable implications for your stream of income.

Table 11c

RRIF Income Comparisons Between Straight-Line Projections and a Balanced Mutual Fund

Age	Fund A Yearly Income (assuming 7% fixed annual return)	Fund B Yearly Income (balanced mutual fund delivering 7% average annual rate of return)*	Percentage Difference in Yearly Income
70	$ 5,000	$ 5,000	0
71	7,515	6,603	−12.1
72	7,566	7,452	−1.5
73	7,619	7,475	−1.9
74	7,671	7,053	−8.1
75	7,732	8,231	6.5
76	7,780	7,016	−9.8
77	7,833	7,708	−1.6
78	7,889	8,606	9.1
79	7,945	8,465	6.5
80	7,999	7,264	−9.2
81	8,047	8,510	5.8
82	8,104	8,738	7.8
83	8,155	7,987	−2.1
84	8,205	7,039	−14.2
85	8,253	7,295	−11.6
86	8,299	8,106	−2.3
87	8,349	7,946	−4.8
88	8,393	5,408	−35.6
89	8,436	6,082	−27.9
90	8,481	6,563	−22.6
91	8,517	5,980	−29.8
92	8,548	6,550	−23.4
93	8,578	7,789	−9.2
94	8,463	8,507	0.5
Total Income	**$ 199,377**	**$ 183,373**	

(assumes a starting balance of 100,000)

* Although the fund delivered a 7% average annual return over the 25-year period, annual returns fluctuated from a high of 25.3% to a low of −25.8%.

Take mutual funds. Many investors are lulled into a false sense of future income stability through their misinterpretation of a fund's average annual returns. While it might make sense, given historical returns, to assume a 7% or 8% average annual return from, say, a Canadian equity mutual fund over a five or 10-year period, it will not deliver a steady return on a year-over-year basis. The more accurate scenario is that the fund's returns will fluctuate, and often quite dramatically, on a consistent basis.

To highlight this point, Table 11c shows the different annual income streams that would be generated within a RRIF by two mutual funds, both with a 25-year average annual return of 7%. Fund A delivers a 7% return each and every year — in other words, a straight-line projection. In contrast, Fund B delivers a 7% average annual return over a 25-year period. Fund A is of necessity fictitious, because, no matter how hard you try, you won't find a mutual fund that delivers a steady 7% annual return year in and year out. But Fund B, the Canadian balanced fund, is the genuine article. Although its annual returns fluctuated from a high of 25.3% to a low of −25.8%, it did deliver an average annual return of 7% over a 25-year period.

When you compare the income streams from an initial investment of $100,000 in funds A and B, based on identical RRIF minimum withdrawal rates, two very different pictures emerge. Fund A, the straight-line projection, delivers a highly predictable dollar amount every year, with the amounts increasing steadily each and every year. The only time that it registers a slight decrease in income is at age 94, when it drops by just over $100 from the preceding year.

Fund B presents a contrasting scenario. Although in the initial years the annual income stream increases fairly steadily, things start to unravel at the age of 76. At that point you would have to deal with a drop in income of $1,215 — to $7,016 from $8,231 in the previous year. There are also declines in income at ages 80, 83, and 84. The most significant drop occurs at age 88, when the annual income falls to $5,408, from $7,946 at age 87 — a difference of over $2,500 (and a difference of closer to $3,000 if you had been relying on your straight-line projections). What's more, annual incomes stay depressed for the following five years, not bouncing back to their previous high until age 94.

The Dangers of Straight-Line Projections

The percentage difference in yearly incomes brings home the dangers of relying too heavily on straight-line projections as an indicator of future RRIF income streams. For 19 of the 25 years, actual yearly incomes would have been less than projected, ranging from differences of –1.5% to –35.6%. As a visual aid, Figure 11a highlights the difference in yearly incomes between using straight-line projections versus actual fund returns.

Figure 11a

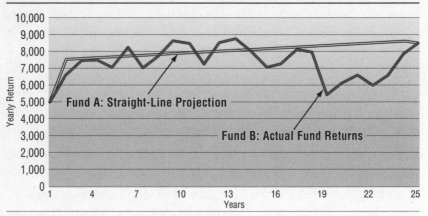

RRIF Income Comparisons: Straight-Line Projections versus Actual Fund Returns

Different Paths

While assuming a 5%, 7%, or 10% average annual rate of return can be useful in arriving at a ballpark figure for the future worth of one's savings, averages can be misleading when it comes to determining income flows. To emphasize this point, Figure 11b plots the different paths the two investments took to deliver a 7% average annual rate of return. Fund A, the fictitious investment, shows up as a nice straight-line projection. An assumption could be made from this projection that future income streams would follow the same trajectory.

In contrast, Fund B — the authentic article — achieved its 7% over the 25-year period with yearly returns that fluctuated between highs of close to 24% to a low of –25.8%. Annual incomes would have varied accordingly. The bottom line is that your income from a RRIF will fluctuate. The degree to which it varies will depend on the investments held and prevailing market conditions.

Figure 11b

Different Paths to a 7% Average Annual Rate of Return

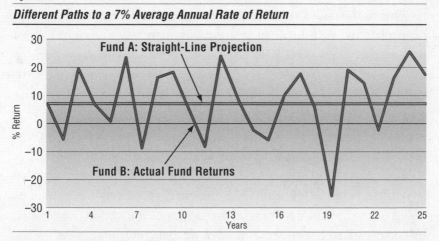

Estate Planning

When it comes to estate planning, RRIFs are really quite flexible. On your death, your spouse can continue to receive the annual minimum payments from the RRIF if, when you set up the plan, you name him or her your *successor annuitant*. If your spouse is named as the beneficiary, the remaining amount may be transferred on a tax-deferred basis to his or her RRIF or, if the spouse is 69 or younger, to his or her RRSP. There are some additional provisions for dependent children. If you have no immediate family, the assets will be paid to your estate or other beneficiaries and taxed accordingly.

To make sure you are making the right decision, and not unknowingly giving a large percentage of your estate to the taxman, you may want to get some professional help.

Planning Ahead

For most people it would be beneficial to delay transferring an RRSP into a RRIF until the deadline date. That way, tax-free compounding can work its magic on the accumulated investments. But planning for this transfer should start well in advance of that date, as there are a number of quite complex issues to consider.

One of the issues you will have to determine, either on your own or, preferably, with some professional guidance, is the right mix of investments for your RRIF. For peace of mind, you may want to move most of your assets into fixed-income investments and drastically reduce your equity holdings. However, for continued growth, you will need optimum exposure to the stock market. What percentage of your portfolio should be in equities will depend, among many other factors, on your other sources of retirement income.

If you are fortunate enough to belong to a defined benefit plan or will receive C/QPP and OAS benefits, those regular payments could be counted as part of your fixed-income allocation. Depending on your retirement income needs and risk tolerance, this would allow you more flexibility when it comes to deciding how much of each asset class, such as bonds or stocks, to hold in your RRIF. You'll find more on how to build a retirement income portfolio in chapters 15 and 16.

All of us, each in our own way, will have to confront the changing face of retirement. With the recent astounding advances in medicine and biotechnology, many of us will live far longer than we ever imagined possible. Whether those years are a time of pleasure and fulfillment or of quiet desperation will depend on many factors. Some issues will be beyond our control, but, with a little planning, securing a comfortable retirement income is certainly well within our grasp.

12

Understanding Locked-In Accounts

*I*f you left a company where you had earned the right to keep your accumulated pension benefits (vesting), you may, like many Canadians have transferred those benefits to a locked-in registered retirement savings plan (RRSP) or a locked-in retirement account (LIRA). Apart from their names, these accounts are almost identical, except for the controls imposed on them by the provinces they operate in.

If your pension money was contributed when you worked in British Columbia, Newfoundland, Nova Scotia, or Ontario, the plan is known as a locked-in RRSP; the other provinces call it a LIRA. The money held in either of these plans is "locked in," so that you cannot withdraw any funds until you reach a certain age. This ensures that the money will be there when you retire. However, the provinces of Ontario and Quebec have eased up on this rule. They now allow limited access to these funds in case of financial hardship or shortened life expectancy.

Until fairly recently, the big drawback of these locked-in accounts was that on retirement you had no option but to purchase an annuity. If your preference was to take some of your savings in cash or if you simply wanted more control over your money, you were out of luck. Now you have a few more choices. You can transfer the investments held in your locked-in account to a life income fund (LIF), or, if you have pension money that was contributed in Alberta, British Columbia, Manitoba, Newfoundland, Ontario, or

Saskatchewan, you have the additional choice of a locked-in retirement income fund (LRIF).

Life Income Funds

A life income fund (LIF) is a fund set up with the proceeds from your locked-in RRSP or LIRA to provide income when you retire. You may also be able to transfer other pension funds into a LIF, depending on the rules of your particular plan. When you open a LIF, you can simply transfer and continue to hold the same investments that you had in your locked-in account. Or you can reallocate your money at any time, typically taking your pick from various investments including GICs, individual bonds and stocks, and mutual funds. If interest rates were high you could also make a decision to purchase an annuity with the proceeds of all or a portion of your LIF.

One of the important benefits of a LIF that is similar to a registered retirement income fund (RRIF) is that all interest income, dividends, and capital gains generated by the investments held in the fund can still continue to grow tax-free. Taxes are paid only on the money you withdraw.

When Can You Open a LIF?

The deadline date for opening a LIF is December 31 of the year in which you turn 69. Of course, you don't have to wait until then to transfer your money. If you need the extra income, you can do it much sooner. However, the earliest date at which you can open a LIF is within 10 years of your normal retirement date under the rules of the originating pension plan (usually 55 years of age). In contrast to a RRIF, you cannot use your spouse's age to determine your withdrawal schedule. Also, you must start taking an income from your LIF one year after you open the plan.

How Much Can You Withdraw?

You can customize the amount you want to withdraw every year, providing that you stay within the minimum and maximum limits set by the Canada Customs and Revenue Agency (CCRA). The minimum withdrawal requirements are the same as for a RRIF (see Chapter 11). The maximum withdrawal amounts are determined by calculating what you would receive if you used the funds in your LIF to purchase a term-certain annuity to age 90 at prevailing interest rates.

Because interest rates and annuity factors change from year to year, so will the maximum withdrawal amounts stipulated for LIFs. These amounts may also differ between provinces, so it's a good idea to check the guidelines with your financial advisor or plan administrator. While the maximum-limit rule on withdrawals may be viewed by some as a punitive measure, its purpose — similar to that of a RRIF — is to ensure that you retain some income for your later years.

If you open a LIF before age 69, you can calculate your minimum annual withdrawal by using a simple formula. Take the value of your LIF at the beginning of the year in which you wish to start withdrawals and divide it by 90 minus your age. Let's say you want to start withdrawals at 65 years of age and have $100,000 in your LIF at the start of that year. The minimum amount you would have to withdraw would be $4,000 ($100,000 ÷ 25). The same formula would apply for each successive year until the required withdrawal rates kicked in.

A Major Drawback

At the end of your 80th year, except in the province of Quebec, you must terminate your LIF and use the proceeds to purchase a life annuity. Even if interest rates are at historical lows or you would prefer to continue making your own investment decisions, you must comply with the regulations. Taking this into consideration, once you get into your mid- or late 70s, if interest rates are high and appear to have peaked, you might want to lock in to those higher interest rates by purchasing an annuity then. (For more on annuities, see Chapter 13.)

Estate Planning

When it comes to estate planning, LIFs are quite flexible. You can transfer the benefits to your spouse on a tax-deferred basis, name a beneficiary, or roll over the LIF into your estate. If you have already converted the proceeds of your LIF into an annuity, then the terms of the particular annuity that you purchased apply.

Locked-in Retirement Income Funds

A locked-in retirement income fund (LRIF) is another more flexible retirement income alternative for people who contributed to a pension plan in Alberta, British Columbia, Manitoba, Newfoundland, Ontario, or Saskatchewan, and who are liquidating their locked-in RRSPs or LIRAs. Although most of the rules for an LRIF are the same as those for a LIF, there are two major differences. Unlike a LIF, an LRIF doesn't have to be converted to an annuity at age 80. You are free to hold whichever investments you choose for as long as you want. Also, the maximum withdrawal requirement for an LRIF provides more flexibility for plan-holders in terms of cash flow.

How Much Can You Withdraw?

With LRIFs you can withdraw either the minimum amount required, which is the same as for LIFs, or a maximum amount that is based on the prior year's investment earnings of the plan. Suppose you had $100,000 in your LRIF at the beginning of 2000 and your investments earned 10% over the year, resulting in an end-of-year balance of $110,000. The minimum you must withdraw in 2001 at, say, age 74 would be 7.71% (see Chapter 11, Table 11a), or $7,710. The maximum you would be allowed to withdraw would be the 10% earnings on your investments, or $10,000.

If you don't need the extra money and decide to withdraw the minimum amount, you can carry forward the difference of 2.29%

to the next year. This gives the plan-holder much more flexibility in terms of cash flow than with a LIF. If you open an LRIF before age 69, you can calculate your minimum annual withdrawal using the formula provided above for LIFs.

Other Key Points

Another important difference between the two plans is that in Ontario a spousal waiver is required before an LRIF can be opened. As there is no survivor protection built into the LRIF, this waiver protects spouses in the event that their partners do not want to designate them as beneficiaries. This means your spouse cannot open a plan and leave the proceeds to someone else without your knowledge. If your spouse wanted to open an LRIF and designate someone other than yourself as the beneficiary, he or she could do so only if you indicated your agreement by signing the spousal waiver.

If you have contributed to a pension plan in Alberta, British Columbia, Manitoba, Newfoundland, Ontario, or Saskatchewan and have already transferred the proceeds to a LIF, you have the option to convert it to an LRIF. However, if you have taken your annual withdrawal entitlement from your LIF, once you convert it to an

Table 12a

Differences Between Life Income Funds (LIFs) and Locked-In Retirement Income Funds (LRIFs)

	LIFs	LRIFs*
Withdrawal restrictions	Min: same as RRIF Max: based on prevailing plan's term-certain annuity rates	Min: same as RRIF Max: based on prior year's investment earnings
Termination regulations	except in province of Quebec, must be terminated by age 80 & proceeds converted to an annuity	none

available only to pension plan contributors in Alberta, British Columbia, Manitoba, Newfoundland, Ontario, and Saskatchewan

LRIF you must wait until the following year before making another withdrawal. This ruling ensures you are not "double-dipping" and depleting your retirement income source.

Table 12a gives a quick overview of the major differences between a life income fund and a locked-in retirement income fund. It's best to get some professional help to decide which option would be best for your own personal circumstances.

Whom to Contact

Your financial advisor or the administrator of your current locked-in RRSP or LIRA should be able to give you all the necessary help and information on transferring your assets to an annuity, a life income fund, or a locked-in retirement income fund.

The Stabilizing Role
of Annuities

Not so long ago, people relied on generous company pension plans and a liberal helping hand from government programs to see them safely through their retirement years. Today circumstances have changed, and these changes are making life in retirement increasingly uncertain for a good many people. In the 1950s and 1960s, Canadians at age 65 could expect to spend an average of seven years in retirement. Now we can expect to spend 20 years or more.

On top of this, fewer workers now have defined benefit pension plans. This was the "old style" pension that guaranteed a retirement income for life. Instead, more and more companies now offer defined contribution plans. These plans take the onus away from the employer and place the investment risk and full responsibility for providing a retirement income on the shoulders of the employees.

Undoubtedly, many people will rise to the challenge and do very well. But what if you are not one of them? What if you invest unwisely or your investments don't produce the income you antici-pated? Well, you can continue to rely on help from government programs, such as C/QPP and OAS — but probably not as much as you would like. At best, it would be prudent to assume that this "helping hand" will waver as the numbers of Canadian seniors swell from under 4 million today to almost 7 million by 2021.

These uncertainties, combined with the possibility that you may have to fund many additional years of retirement living, raise many *issues. Will your investment choices guarantee you a stable and adequate income over a 20-year, 30-year, or even longer retirement? Could you financially ride out a prolonged downturn in the markets? Would you worry yourself sick every time your investments declined in value? If these questions make you feel a bit weak at the knees, you may want to consider stabilizing your retirement income by stashing part of your nest egg in an annuity.*

All about Annuities

An annuity is simply a contract between you and an insurance company or financial institution by which you give the company some or all of your retirement savings. In exchange, they agree to pay you a guaranteed sum of money each month for a certain period of time — usually for life. In order to determine what this amount will be, the actuaries at the company go to work, considering what return they will get on your lump-sum payment of, say, $50,000 or $100,000, and how long you want the payments to continue. Typically, your money will be invested in conservative investments that are sensitive to interest rates. This means that the higher the long-term interest rates are when you purchase the annuity, the larger your monthly cheque will be, since the annuity issuer can get a better return on your money. Conversely, the lower those interest rates are, the smaller your payments.

They also have to determine for how long your annuity payments might have to be made. Or, to put it bluntly, how long it will be before you die. The longer your life expectancy, the smaller your payments. This is where women pay the price. A woman won't receive as high a payment as her same-age male counterpart, simply because women have longer life expectancies. The shorter your life expectancy, the higher your payments will be. This higher payout has nothing to do with investment performance; it's simply because the insurance company expects to make payments for fewer years.

If you outlive their life-expectancy projection, then the company loses money because it will have to make payments for longer than it expected. If, however, you die earlier than anticipated, the company gains. They get to keep the remainder of the annuity proceeds. In order to avoid such wide variations in returns, insurance companies spread the investment risk among as many annuity buyers as possible. That way their gains from annuitants who die early balance out their losses from those who outlive their life expectancies.

The Different Types of Annuities

The four main types of annuities are life, joint-and-last-survivor, guaranteed term, and term-certain. Which one is right for you will depend on your health, your family circumstances, your other sources of retirement income, and your feelings about financial security.

Life annuities can be purchased only through a life insurance company. With this type of annuity, you will receive a fixed regular payment for as long as you live. Even if you live to 110, far beyond what the insurance company expects, you will still get your regular cheque. That's the good news. The bad news is that on your death, whether it occurs in your 80s or your 90s or a month after you buy the annuity, the payments stop and the insurance company keeps whatever principal is left. No funds will be transferred to your spouse, your dependants, or your estate.

You might consider this type of annuity if your other sources of guaranteed retirement income are limited, you are in good health, your parents lived to a ripe old age, and you have no dependants or they have other, adequate sources of income.

Joint-and-last-survivor annuities are geared towards married couples. They pay a set amount throughout both spouses' lifetimes. They are typically structured to give higher payments while both spouses are alive and smaller payments (around 60%) to the surviving spouse. When both spouses have died, payments stop, and the insurance company keeps whatever principal is left, if any. This type of annuity may be a good choice if you and your spouse are both in good health and the guarantee of keeping monthly benefits flowing for the surviving spouse is important to you.

Guaranteed term annuities may be an option if you want to leave something to your heirs. These annuities provide payments for a certain period, for example, a 10- or 15-year term. If you die before those 10 or 15 years are up, the insurance company will give the remaining payments to your spouse or an equivalent lump-sum value to your estate. This guarantee, though, will result in smaller payments, as a guaranteed period completely eliminates the chance that the insurer could pay out for fewer years. Of course, if you live longer than the term covered, all payments cease.

Term-certain annuities are sold by insurance companies and financial institutions, and guarantee payments until you reach 90 years of age, at which time all payments cease. If you die earlier, payments continue to be paid to your surviving spouse until the year in which you would have turned 90. If you have no surviving spouse, the remaining payments are cashed out and a lump sum is paid to your estate.

Tables 13a and 13b will give you some idea of the differences in monthly and annual payments among joint, female, and male annuitants from straight life annuities and from those with a 10-year guaranteed term. As you will see, you end up with slightly lower payouts from an annuity with a guaranteed term. However, regardless of whether it is a life or guaranteed-term annuity, male annuitants get the highest payouts, followed by females and then couples.

Advantages and Disadvantages

The big benefit of an annuity is that it will provide you with retirement income for as long as you live, or over the period of time you wish covered. Other advantages include not having to make ongoing

Table 13a

Average Monthly Annuity Payments

Type of Annuity	Age of Annuitant					
	55	60	65	70	75	80
Life annuity						
Joint	$ 512	$ 542	$ 584	$ 643	$ 730	$ 844
Female	548	589	646	721	836	988
Male	589	642	717	814	956	1,133
Life annuity with 10-year term guarantee						
Joint	510	539	582	639	716	806
Female	524	580	631	695	778	863
Male	578	625	686	757	837	909

(based on a $100,000 investment in an annuity; payout rates as of November 2001)

Table 13b

Average Annual Annuity Income

Type of Annuity	Age of Annuitant					
	55	60	65	70	75	80
Life annuity						
Joint	$ 6,138	$ 6,500	$ 7,011	$ 7,716	$ 8,761	$ 10,122
Female	6,580	7,065	7,747	8,646	10,033	11,855
Male	7,072	7,706	8,604	9,763	11,471	13,598
Life annuity with 10-year term guarantee						
Joint	6,114	6,474	6,987	7,665	8,592	9,675
Female	6,510	6,959	7,570	8,342	9,332	10,360
Male	6,939	7,500	8,227	9,082	10,042	10,905

(based on a $100,000 investment in an annuity; payout rates as of November 2001)

management or investment decisions and freedom from anxiety about stock market crashes or interest rate declines. You also have some flexibility over the size of payments. As you can see in tables 13a and 13b, the older you are before you purchase an annuity, and the fewer frills you want, the higher your payments will be. And, as mentioned earlier, if you are a male, your payouts will be higher because of your shorter life expectancy.

The major disadvantage of purchasing an annuity is loss of principal. Once you have paid out that $50,000 or $150,000, that money is gone. If you need money to cover major home repairs or other unexpected expenses, you cannot withdraw additional amounts. You are also locked in; if interest rates increase, you cannot switch to a new annuity that makes higher payments. Also, annuity payments are rarely indexed to keep pace with inflation. This means that with most types of annuities you will receive the same dollar payment when you are 80 years of age as you will when you are 90. However, insurance companies and financial institutions will undoubtedly be bringing many new products into the marketplace to meet the needs of the growing senior population.

The latest model to hit Wall Street is an immediate-variable annuity. This type of annuity spreads your savings among an assortment of mutual funds that will provide a growing stream of income. The size of the monthly cheque would vary depending on various factors such as age, sex, amount invested, and the assumed investment return. But while it's certainly helpful for consumers to have more choice, it's important to keep in mind that they will all come with an appropriate price tag.

Is an Annuity for You?

Clearly you should avoid annuities if your life expectancy is poor. You also probably shouldn't buy one until later in your retirement. There are a couple of reasons for this. First, the older you are when you purchase an annuity, the higher the income stream. Second, if you have retirement savings in a registered retirement income fund, at 77 years of age the minimum withdrawal limit from a RRIF starts to exceed 8% a year. If your investments are returning less than that, then your capital will steadily decrease. At that point you may want to use some of the proceeds of your RRIF or locked-in retirement income fund (LRIF) to buy an annuity. If your money is in a life income fund (LIF), then of course you don't have an option. Those accounts must be terminated at age 80 and the proceeds used to purchase an annuity.

Deciding whether or not to purchase an annuity is not easy. There are a number of important issues to be addressed, but the following statements may point you in the right direction. If you tend to agree with them, then purchasing an annuity may be a good choice for you. But, as this is an extremely important and irreversible decision, you should make it only with the help of a qualified professional such as your accountant or financial advisor.

- I am in good health, with a family history of longevity.
- I am concerned about outliving my retirement savings.
- I want to ensure a guaranteed retirement income for the rest of my life or for a specific term.
- After I retire, I want to make fewer investment decisions.
- I am not very concerned about leaving an inheritance.

It Pays to Shop Around

Payments from an annuity are counted as taxable income and can be received on a monthly, quarterly, or annual basis, whichever suits you best. As the payments, as well as rates and options for annuities, can vary quite substantially from company to company, it's worthwhile to comparison shop and find the one that best fits your needs.

As can be seen in Table 13c, payouts from various companies from a straight life annuity (based on a $100,000 investment) at age 65 range for females from a low of $607 a month to a high of $695, for males from $676 to $772, and for couples from $552 to $617. Although the differences might not seem hugely significant when viewed from the standpoint of monthly income, they become extremely important over, say, a 25-year retirement period. In the case of a female, the $552 monthly payment provides a total retirement income of about $182,000 to age 90, while the monthly payment of $695 provides $208,500 — for a very significant difference of $26,500 in total retirement income.

Table 13c

Monthly Payout Ranges from a Straight Life Annuity at Age 65

	High	Low
Joint	$ 617	$ 552
Female	695	607
Male	772	676

(based on a $100,000 investment in an annuity; payout rates as of November 2001)

The older you are before buying an annuity, the greater the differences become. At age 80, the payout for females ranges from $882 to $1,084, for males from $922 to $1,258, and for couples from $759 to $884. Assuming they live to reach 90 years of age, women end up with a total retirement income for the 10-year period ranging from $106,000 to $130,000; for men it's from just over $110,000 to close to $151,000. For couples, it ranges from a low of $91,000 to a high of $106,000. As is to be expected, payments from annuities with a 10-year guaranteed term are lower across the board.

Check It Out

It is a very good idea to make certain that the company you choose is reputable and financially sound and has an unblemished record when it comes to meeting its obligations — in other words, a top-rated company. Insurance rating agencies such as Standard & Poor's and Moody's grade the financial strength of these companies, and they award their highest rating of AAA to only the top insurance companies. Your financial advisor or insurance agent should be able to help you in this area.

Living Longer and Living Better: The Keys to a Financially Secure Retirement

5

14

Beating the Odds:
Ensuring an Income for Life

Once you have accumulated your retirement savings, there are a couple of important issues that ultimately have to be addressed. And we are not talking about where you are going to live or how you are going to fill your time. However, the answer to both those questions could be dramatically affected by how you resolve the following, much more important ones: How much can you safely withdraw each year without running the risk of depleting your savings in your lifetime? And, should you take a percentage withdrawal or a fixed dollar amount?

Although, we have no control over when a bear or bull market will strike, or over interest rate fluctuations, the inflation rate, recessions, wars, or the weather, we do have control over how much or how little we withdraw. At the end of the day, this is the highest risk factor a retiree faces, and the only decision over which he or she has any say.

Will Your Money Last?

Obviously, if you have $100,000 in your retirement nest egg and you want to take out $25,000 a year, it's not going to last very long. You don't need to run a complicated computer program to come to that conclusion — common sense will do the trick. But what if you wanted to withdraw $6,000 or $7,000 a year? How long would your $100,000 last? On the other hand, would you be better off using a fixed percentage withdrawal rate based on the starting balance? Or does it really make any difference? And what about inflation?

The Perils of Inflation

Inflation — the rise over time in the average price of goods and services — is something that all retirees have to factor into their plans. Why? Because it can steadily erode the purchasing power of their income, posing one of the biggest threats to their financial security. An income that's comfortable at retirement today could well prove to be insufficient a few years from now because, as the cost of living rises, one's money buys less over time.

For example, over the 30 years between 1970 and 2000, inflation in Canada averaged 5.3%. What this means is that a basket of goods and services that cost $100 in 1970 would have escalated to $465 by the end of that period. In terms of purchasing power, inflation would have cut the value of $100 to $21.50 over the same 30 years. So someone retiring in 1970 on a fixed monthly pension that was not indexed to inflation would have seen his or her standard of living fall by close to 80% by the year 2000!

Although inflation has been relatively tame over the past decade, averaging 1.6% since 1992, no one can predict the direction or rate of inflation in the future. As retirees and others on fixed incomes are particularly vulnerable to its effects, it's prudent to take inflation into account when projecting future retirement income streams.

Percentage Versus Dollar Withdrawals: A Real-World Case Study

The illustrations on page 126 and page 128 (tables 14a and 14b) assume a starting balance of $100,000 invested in a balanced mutual fund holding both stocks and bonds. They show how the two different withdrawal strategies, fixed-dollar and fixed-percentage, would have fared over the 30-year period from 1970 to 2000. To depict as accurate a picture as possible, real fund data has been utilized. Although the actual average annualized compound rate of return of the fund over the entire 30-year period was 9.1%, returns ranged from a high of 31% to a low of –19%. Moreover, the fund posted negative returns for nine of the 30 years.

Along with the specific fund data, it is important to get some perspective on the major economic and political events that provided the backdrop for the period. From 1970 to 2000, the Canadian economy experienced three recessions — one for each decade: 1973–74, 1981–82, and 1990–91 — as well as a period of double-digit inflation, and soaring interest rates in the early 1980s. We also experienced the 1990 Gulf War, the Asian currency crisis of 1998, the Y2K scare, a record stock market crash in 1987, the break-up of the Soviet Union, and the quadrupling of oil prices in the 1970s. In other words, it was a fairly normal 30-year span. Although no one can predict the future, these events should give some indication of what might lie ahead. In all probability, it will include more of the same, with its share of bull and bear markets, economic booms and periods of recession, trade agreements, and wars.

Fixed-Dollar Retirement Incomes

Table 14a shows fixed-dollar retirement income streams, based on withdrawals of $5,000, $7,000, and $9,000 a year, that would be generated from a starting balance of $100,000 over the 30 years from 1970 to 2000. The income stream is also indexed to a 3% rate of inflation, which represents the long-term average annual increase in consumer prices. In this illustration, the dollar amount withdrawn is thus increased by 3% every year to compensate for rising prices. Consequently, in Year 2 an income of $5,000 would rise to $5,150 ($5,000 + 3%), the income in Year 3 would rise to $5,305 ($5,150 +3%), and so forth.

As you can see, the $5,000 strategy generates the highest total withdrawal amount of $238,000 and also leaves $238,000 in the kitty to pass on to one's heirs. More important, of the three examples it is the only one to survive the 30-year period. Opting to take

Table 14a

Fixed Dollar Retirement Incomes Indexed to Inflation

Year	Annual Income	Year-end Balance	Annual Income	Year-end Balance	Annual Income	Year-end Balance
1	$ 5,000	$ 93,828	$ 7,000	$ 91,828	$ 9,000	$ 89,828
2	5,150	96,746	7,210	92,514	9,270	88,282
3	5,305	108,145	7,426	101,061	9,548	93,977
4	5,464	97,572	7,649	88,637	9,835	79,702
5	5,628	73,442	7,879	63,950	10,130	54,459
6	5,796	80,244	8,115	66,806	10,433	53,367
7	5,970	83,393	8,358	66,039	10,746	48,685
8	6,149	77,051	8,609	57,277	11,069	37,504
9	6,334	83,292	8,867	57,758	11,401	32,224
10	6,524	98,710	9,133	63,840	11,743	28,969
11	6,720	113,548	9,407	68,374	12,095	23,201
12	6,921	101,660	9,690	55,694	12,458	9,728
13	7,129	110,996	9,980	54,734	11,303	0
14	7,343	138,044	10,280	61,413	0	0
15	7,563	126,068	10,588	48,861	0	0
16	7,790	143,150	10,906	47,595	0	0
17	8,024	142,695	11,233	38,879	0	0
18	8,264	141,231	11,570	29,162	0	0
19	8,512	149,480	11,917	20,705	0	0
20	8,768	163,665	12,275	11,610	0	0
21	9,031	144,262	10,874	0	0	0
22	9,301	156,810	0	0	0	0
23	9,581	153,405	0	0	0	0
24	9,868	186,183	0	0	0	0
25	10,164	174,467	0	0	0	0
26	10,469	185,863	0	0	0	0
27	10,783	207,225	0	0	0	0
28	11,106	222,202	0	0	0	0
29	11,440	208,369	0	0	0	0
30	11,783	237,806	0	0	0	0
Total	$ 237,877		$ 198,967		$ 139,032	

(assumes a $100,000 starting balance and a 3% annual rate of inflation; projected retirement income streams use actual fund returns from a balanced mutual fund that posted an annual compound return of 9.1% over the 30-year period from 1970 to 2000)

out $7,000 or $9,000 would have depleted your capital in 21 years for the former and in only 13 years for the latter.

The message for retirees is that the higher the dollar withdrawal, the greater the risk of running out of money. The only way to offset this is to accumulate considerably more assets.

Fixed-Percentage Retirement Incomes

In contrast, Table 14b shows the income streams based on fixed-percentage withdrawals of 5%, 7%, and 9% a year that would be generated from a starting balance of $100,000 over the 30-year period. The first thing you will notice is that, regardless of the percent withdrawn, you will never run out of money. Of course, the higher the balance, the higher the income, and conversely, the lower the balance, the lower the income. Moreover, annual incomes will also fluctuate because of the annual returns of the underlying investment — in this case, a balanced mutual fund.

In this illustration, the 5% withdrawal rate generates a rising stream of income, whereas with the 9% rate, the income stream is fairly steady. However, in the first year the 5% withdrawal provides an income of only $4,941, whereas the 9% rate yields an income of $8,895, or 80% more. But in the 30th year the 5% rate would provide an income of $15,368, compared with only $7,945 for the 9% withdrawal rate. The 5% rate also leaves a 30-year end balance of $291,987, compared to $154,221 for the 7% rate and $80,334 for the 9% withdrawal rate.

Table 14c shows the average annual retirement income generated by each fixed-percentage withdrawal during the three decades from 1970 to 2000. Under the 5% withdrawal rate, average annual incomes rise from $4,903 in the first 10 years to $8,211 for the second 10-year period to $12,097 in the final decade. With a 7% withdrawal rate, average annual incomes increase similarly, rising from around $6,250 a year in the first decade to close to $10,000 by the third decade. On the other hand, with the 9% withdrawal rate, the average annual income is fairly steady, at around $7,500 for each decade.

Table 14b

Fixed-Percentage Retirement Income Flows

Year	Annual Income (5% withdrawal rate)	Year-end Balance	Annual Income (7% withdrawal rate)	Year-end Balance	Annual Income (9% withdrawal rate)	Year-end Balance
1	$ 4,941	$ 93,887	$ 6,918	$ 91,910	$ 8,895	$ 89,933
2	5,098	96,861	6,987	92,826	8,790	88,876
3	5,679	107,906	7,620	101,234	9,380	94,842
4	5,140	97,667	6,752	89,699	8,132	82,228
5	3,957	75,190	5,088	67,601	5,997	60,638
6	4,404	83,684	5,544	73,654	6,394	64,647
7	4,660	88,533	5,742	76,282	6,479	65,514
8	4,416	83,913	5,327	70,779	5,883	59,480
9	4,880	92,727	5,763	76,567	6,227	62,961
10	5,858	111,296	6,772	89,965	7,159	72,387
11	6,780	128,822	7,673	101,940	7,938	80,258
12	6,159	117,029	6,824	90,658	6,907	69,841
13	6,799	129,184	7,374	97,967	7,304	73,848
14	8,460	160,749	8,982	119,338	8,706	88,023
15	7,781	147,830	8,087	107,436	7,669	77,540
16	8,850	168,145	9,004	119,628	8,355	84,483
17	8,852	168,183	8,817	117,136	8,005	80,944
18	8,810	167,388	8,590	114,128	7,632	77,169
19	9,363	177,890	8,937	118,735	7,769	78,558
20	10,260	194,946	9,588	127,380	8,156	82,465
21	9,130	173,461	8,351	110,956	6,951	70,287
22	9,987	189,746	8,943	118,817	7,284	73,649
23	9,861	187,358	8,645	114,852	6,889	69,660
24	11,972	227,471	10,275	136,505	8,012	81,013
25	11,279	214,295	9,476	125,891	7,230	73,107
26	12,058	229,094	9,917	131,752	7,404	74,865
27	13,436	255,280	10,818	143,720	7,903	79,909
28	14,371	273,042	11,327	150,484	8,097	81,870
29	13,505	256,596	10,420	138,443	7,289	73,700
30	15,368	291,987	11,608	154,221	7,945	80,334
Total	**$ 252,114**		**$ 246,167**		**$ 226,783**	

(assumes a $100,000 starting balance; projected retirement income streams use actual fund returns from a balanced mutual fund that posted an annual compound return of 9.1% over the 30-year period from 1970 to 2000)

Table 14c

**Average Annual Retirement Incomes under
Different Percentage Withdrawal Rates**

	5%	7%	9%
Decade 1	$ 4,903	$ 6,251	$ 7,334
Decade 2	8,211	8,388	7,844
Decade 3	12,097	9,978	7,500

(assumes a $100,000 starting balance)

Mid-Course Adjustments

Of course, results would vary depending on the underlying investment and the returns it delivered over the period in question. In addition, there is also room to manoeuvre. Inflation could be factored in every two or three years instead of every year, and a healthy increase in principal in any given year could allow higher withdrawals. What's more, retirees who do not wish to leave an estate could quite comfortably increase their income in later years. However, the foregoing should help to illustrate what one can reasonably expect under different scenarios.

The 5% Rule

Numerous studies have been conducted with historical data to back-test the sustainability of retirement income flows using different variables. These variables include different withdrawal rates, payout periods, asset allocations, and historical annual return data, including and excluding the Great Depression. Monte Carlo simulations randomly draw on the different variables to construct a single test. The process is then repeated thousands of times and the results are summarized, providing a quantitative estimate of the range and distribution of all possible returns. The aim of these simulations is to test the survival rate of a portfolio in different scenarios and to identify the ones that have the best chance for success.

In a 1998 study, *Retirement Savings: Choosing a Withdrawal Rate That Is Sustainable*, professors Philip Cooley, Carl Hubbard, and Daniel Walz of Trinity University in San Antonio, Texas, found that for withdrawal periods longer than 15 years, withdrawal rates exceeding 5% dramatically reduced the probability of success. The study went on to emphasize the need for conservative withdrawal rates and, by implication, more savings to provide a comfortable retirement.

Other similar studies concur that

- a "safe" withdrawal rate ranges between 4% to 6% of a retiree's starting portfolio;
- fixed-dollar withdrawals increase investment risk and the possibility of liquidating one's portfolio during prolonged market declines;
- given the choice between investments with high volatility and those with low volatility, all else being equal (rate of return, cost, etc.), the investment with the lower volatility will significantly reduce the possibility that a retiree's nest egg will implode.

Do not make the mistake of underestimating the importance of selecting a reasonable withdrawal rate, given the capital available. If you have not accumulated enough, you may be tempted either to withdraw more money or to invest in riskier assets in order to provide a higher return. Both courses of action will in all likelihood increase your chances of running out of money.

Although living on 4% or 5% of your retirement savings probably sounds pretty dismal, it's important to bear in mind that this is just one source of retirement income. Most Canadians will qualify for Old Age Security benefits, and workers who have paid into the C/QPP will be eligible for retirement benefits. Moreover, percentage withdrawals from registered plans, such as registered retirement income funds, gradually increase over time, so savings in those plans should generate more income as the years pass.

15

Building a
Retirement Income Portfolio

When you retire, you might live another 20 to 30 years. That's the
good news. But it could also be the bad news if your income
steadily declines over the years. The only way to guard against this
slow deterioration of your standard of living is to maintain some
exposure to stocks. Yes, we all agree they can be unpredictable, but
then again they do provide that essential component for any effec-
tive retirement portfolio — growth.

The Role of Stocks and Bonds

There's a big difference between a regular source of retirement
income, such as a CPP or defined benefit cheque, and income from
sources that are less certain, such as investments. That's a big
dilemma for retirees. On the one hand, conservative investments
such as guaranteed investment certificates (GICs) or Government of
Canada bonds, which carry little or no risk, look very appealing.
But while they may give you peace of mind, they probably won't
provide enough income over the long term to meet your needs.
After all, with a five-year GIC currently yielding about 4%, a
$200,000 portfolio would provide an income of only $8,000 in the
first year of retirement. If you needed more, you'd have to sell some
bonds. That, combined with the effects of inflation, would eat away
at your principal and further jeopardize your future income stream.

If your investments are held outside a registered plan, you can count on taxes also taking their toll. For example, if your invest-ments earn 4%, after taxes (assuming a 36% tax rate) you would be left with 2.6%. And after an inflation rate of, say, 3% is factored in, you are actually in a loss position, at –0.4%. In dollar terms, a $1,000 investment earning 4% would grow to $1,040 at the end of the first year. After taxes, you would be left with $1,026, and after inflation, your original $1,000 investment would have shrunk to $995. As you can see, the combined effects of inflation and taxes can wreak havoc on your savings.

Once you are retired and relying on getting additional income from your investments, your goal is to make sure that the stream of income is as generous and dependable as possible. Of course, you would like to achieve this with no risk to your capital, but unless you have a couple of million stashed away to maintain that higher stream of income, you will need to hold stocks that historically have outpaced bonds by about 5% and inflation by close to 8% a year.

The Inflation Factor

The simplest interpretation of the effects of inflation is that, as time goes by, prices are inclined to rise. In other words, your dollar is worth less. As the years pass, increases in living costs can slowly but relentlessly eat away at your purchasing power and your standard of living.

If you look at Table 15a, you will see how even a 3% rate of inflation — the historical average for Canada since the First World War — can cut the value of a dollar by almost 15% in the space of only five years. While that may not sound like much, you might want to contemplate what happens to the value of $2,000 if it sud-denly drops to $1,700. And that decline in purchasing power is over only five years. Over 25 years, the effects are even more devastating — a 3% rate of inflation cuts the value of a dollar in half! Twenty-five years down the road, your $100,000 today will be worth less than $50,000.

Some people argue that, because retirees of the past have not

Table 15a

Inflation and the Purchasing Power of One Dollar

	Average Annual Rate of Inflation			
Years	2%	3%	4%	5%
0	$ 1.00	$ 1.00	$ 1.00	$ 1.00
5	0.90	0.86	0.82	0.78
15	0.74	0.64	0.55	0.48
25	0.60	0.48	0.38	0.30

typically bought big-ticket items, factoring in a 1% rate of inflation is more than adequate. But the very nature of retirement is undergoing crucial changes because of measurable factors such as increased longevity, and less tangible elements, such as heightened expectations. There are not many future retirees who are prepared, like past generations, to live quietly and make do with what they have. Banking on a 1% rate of inflation indicates an ill-founded belief that today's baby-boom "wantaholics" will quietly metamorphose into tomorrow's frugal seniors.

On the plus side, the CPP and OAS, and also some defined benefit plans, are indexed to the cost of living. So you won't have to worry about the effects of inflation on those benefits, unless, of course, you have doubts about the future viability of the government programs. Maybe it's simply best to take steps now to guard against the effect of inflation on your future retirement income. Otherwise, you may be forced to adopt what could be a very Spartan lifestyle, perhaps not early on in retirement, but certainly as the years pass.

To offset the effects of inflation, your income needs to keep pace. Assuming that you neither re-enter the workforce in your chosen profession nor become a fast-food elder, this income will have to be generated from a pool of assets that continues to grow — which means that some of those assets will have to be stocks.

Building a Portfolio for Maximum Growth and Income

Similarly to when you were working, in your retirement you need to hold a diversified portfolio of assets in order to meet your goals. Most retirees want a certain level of safety, current income to meet their living expenses, and some capital growth. How much you allocate to each objective will depend on your individual needs and how much or how little income you expect to receive from other sources.

The average combined benefits from CPP and OAS are currently about $840 a month; if you are fortunate enough to qualify for the maximum payouts, you will get around $1,220. Add on any other guaranteed income, such as a pension from a defined benefit plan, and this total will form the basis of your retirement income. If it is not enough to meet your living expenses, the remainder will have to be generated from your investments.

The first priority for any retirement portfolio is to secure your additional income needs for the first three to five years. This is money that should not be exposed to any risk; it should be held in secure and conservative investments. Options include money-market funds, or "laddering" a series of investments such as GICs or bonds so that they mature in different years, rolling them over regularly.

Another option is to use some of your savings to purchase an annuity that would give you an additional fixed stream of income. A typical monthly payout on a $100,000 life annuity at age 65 would be around $720 if you are male, $645 for a female, or about $585 for a couple (for more on annuities, see Chapter 13).

Once you have determined how much to set aside to meet your living expenses, the remainder of your assets should be split, according to your risk tolerance, between fixed-income investments and stocks. The income from these investments could be used to pay for vacations or unexpected expenses, and to reinvest. Reinvesting some — or all, if you don't need the additional income — of your gains allows your assets to continue to grow. Considering that some of us will live to become centenarians, this growth will be crucial in ensuring that the money lasts.

As a rough guideline, if your guaranteed retirement income (such as the CPP, OAS, or a defined benefit plan) is more than adequate to cover all your living expenses, you could consider allocating a higher proportion of your investments to individual stocks or stock mutual funds. On the other hand, if you need to rely on your savings to provide the lion's share of your living costs in retirement, you have to adopt a more cautious investment strategy. A conservative portfolio with a higher weighting in fixed-income investments would provide the required stability and income — but some exposure to stocks would still be essential to provide the necessary growth element.

Estate Planning

Another point, and an important one for many people, is whether or not you want to leave any money or other assets to family members or others. If you do, it's crucial that you have a valid will that will ensure your assets are distributed efficiently and according to your wishes. That's the easy part. The hard part is making sure that you have also protected your assets, as much as humanly possible, from the potential tax consequences. Otherwise, when you die, the proceeds of your estate will be treated as taxable income, and significant amounts could be lost to taxes.

Designating your spouse or, if they meet the necessary requirements, your dependent children as your RRSP or RRIF beneficiaries ensures that no taxes are paid on those assets until the funds are withdrawn. It's important to get advice from a professional, such as your lawyer, accountant, financial advisor, or insurance agent, if you want to ensure that "little something" doesn't end up as next to nothing!

16

Strategic Retirement Portfolios: A Sound Approach to Investing

As investors are now beginning to realize, building and maintaining a retirement portfolio isn't easy. The unprecedented bull market of the 1990s lulled many into believing that continued double-digit returns would be the norm. But the meltdown of the NASDAQ and the sharp downturn in major equity markets have served as a cruel wake-up call, alerting all but the most sanguine of investors to the harsh reality that their portfolios need ongoing tending.

In hindsight, many investors are now realizing that their retirement portfolios were far too aggressive and significantly out of line with their true risk tolerance. Unfortunately for those who are approaching retirement, this could have significant and lasting implications for their future retirement income potential. To understand the full importance of asset allocation, let's go back in time and look at how two investors with identical retirement goals — but very different portfolios — fared during the stock market crash of 1987.

Confronting the Bear

Back in 1987, two investors, Mr. A and Ms. B, each had accumulated retirement savings of $100,000 and were planning to retire in 1992. Over the intervening five years, Mr. A decided to hold on to his aggressive portfolio, which had an asset allocation of 80%

stocks and 20% bonds. In contrast, Ms. B shifted to a more conservative portfolio of 80% bonds and 20% stocks. Table 16a shows the impact of the 1987 bear market on both portfolios. In the year that they planned to retire, Mr. A ended up with the grand total of $118,700, and Ms. B with $168,800 — a difference of $50,100.

Table 16a

Impact of the 1987 Bear Market on Retirement Savings:
Target Retirement Date of Five Years, 1987–92

	Investor A	Investor B
Portfolio	80% stocks/20% bonds	20% stocks/80% bonds
Starting balance	$ 100,000	$ 100,000
Ending balance	$ 118,700	$ 168,800
Average annual return	3.5%	11.0%
Cumulative return	18.7%	68.8%

The 1987 bear market lasted for four months; during this period the TSE 300 Total Return Index declined by more than 25%. The index plunged by 22.5% in the month of October alone, registering the sharpest monthly decline in the stock market since the Great Depression of the 1930s. It took two years for the market to recover and regain its losses but, with the onset of the 1990–91 recession, the TSE again came under considerable downward pressure.

The index fell by a further 18% in 1990. The upshot is, for the five-year period from July 1987 to July 1992 — the year our intrepid investors were retiring — the TSE 300 recorded an average annual return of only 0.4%. A $100,000 investment in the stock market in July 1987 would have grown to a paltry $102,000 by July 1992.

While no one can predict when a bear market will strike, we have to accept that market corrections are part and parcel of the investing scene. Before we get overly uneasy, however, history shows that positive market movements have significantly outweighed the negative ones. For example, for the 81-year period stretching from 1920 to 2000, the TSE 300 posted positive returns for 54 of the years and negative returns for only 27. During this period, returns averaged 17% during the up years and –12.2% during the down years.

After the Bear

And what would the outcome be for Mr. A and Ms. B in retirement? Assuming a 7% annual rate of return and a 25-year time line with a zero ending balance, Mr. A's retirement nest egg of $118,700 would generate a monthly income of about $825, or $9,875 a year. Ms. B is in much better shape. Her starting retirement balance of $168,800 will give her a monthly income of $1,170, or $14,040 a year for 25 years (see Table 16b.) Over the entire 25-year period, Ms. B can withdraw a total of $351,000, whereas Mr. A's total withdrawals will amount to only $247,000 — a difference of over $104,000. By shifting to a conservative portfolio prior to retirement, Ms. B weathered the 1987 bear market and ended up with a monthly income stream that was 40% higher than Mr. A's.

Table 16b

Impact of the 1987 Bear Market on Retirement Incomes

	Investor A	Investor B
Starting balance	$ 118,700	$ 168,800
Withdrawals		
Monthly income	$ 825	$ 1,170
Annual income	$ 9,875	$ 14,040

The bottom-line is that nobody knows when a bear market will strike. So playing "retirement roulette" with your savings is not a game that you want to indulge in. The consequences could be irrevocable.

A Strategic Retirement: Don't Worry, Be Secure

Most people spend at least some time figuring out the appropriate asset mix they need in order to accumulate money for their retirement — the growth phase — and, hopefully, an equal amount of time and effort selecting the right mix of investments for the income phase. What they don't spend any time on is the necessary gradual shift of investments over the years from the one type of asset allocation to the other.

In many cases, individuals simply wait until the date of their retirement to move their assets from their savings plan to their income fund. It's possible that their mixture of stocks and fixed-income investments is quite suitable. If it is, and they are faced with a bear market in the years before their retirement, while they might be upset, it won't seriously derail their future income plans.

But what if, through over-optimism, neglect, or inexperience, their asset allocation is no longer suitable? What if the stock component should have been substantially reduced? A bear market will certainly have serious and lasting implications for their future retirement income stream. If you are nodding your head in agreement at this point, then you may want to consider a strategic retirement portfolio.

Strategic retirement planning is a long-term investment approach that emphasizes risk reduction by gradually shifting from aggressive to more conservative investments throughout an individual's working years. At the onset, instead of focusing on the investor's risk tolerance — which, let's face it, tends to go up and down like an umbrella according to prevailing conditions — the asset mix is based on the actual planned date of retirement and presumes a certain level of risk based on the time left until that date. In this way, investors with later retirement target dates can invest very aggressively, because, with a longer investment time horizon, their portfolios are capable of absorbing short-term volatility.

As the investor gets closer to his or her retirement year, the assets are gradually shifted to more conservative investments. Because no one can foresee when a bear market will hit, this systematic and gradual notching-down of one's asset allocation from aggressive to conservative, especially in the five to 10 years before retirement, is a prudent strategy.

As you will see from Tables 16c and 16d, someone who plans to retire in, say, 25 years would choose either the maximum growth portfolio (100% stocks) or the growth portfolio (80% stocks/20% bonds). With such a long investment horizon, their portfolio will have plenty of time to recover from any down markets. Individuals with a retirement target date of, say, 15 years should choose between the growth (80% stocks/20% bonds) and balanced (60% stocks/40% bonds) portfolios. Those retiring in 10 to 15 years could opt for the balanced portfolio (60% stocks/40% bonds) or the conservative portfolio (40% stocks/60% bonds).

Table 16c

Retirement investment horizons

Years to Retirement	Suggested Portfolios
20+	maximum growth/growth
15+	growth/balanced
10+	balanced/conservative
5+	conservative/income
5–	income

Table 16d

Asset Allocation

	Stocks	Bonds	Average Annual Return (1926–2000)	Worst Annual Loss (1926–2000)
Maximum growth	100%	0%	11.0%	−43.1%
Growth	80	20	10.3	−34.9
Balanced	60	40	9.3	−26.6
Conservative	40	60	8.2	−18.4
Income	20	80	7.0	−10.1

(stocks: S&P 500; bonds: long-term U.S. corporate bonds)

Individuals with between five and 10 years to retirement are getting ever closer to their target date. They have the option of two portfolios: conservative (40% stocks/60% bonds) or income (20% stocks/80% bonds). The income portfolio would be suitable for someone with less than five years until retirement.

Table 16d gives the annual average return for each portfolio and its worst annual loss over the period from 1926 to 2000. While there is no guarantee that these results will be repeated in future years — they may be better or worse — they can serve as a general guide.

Once investors have been slotted into the appropriate time frame, their investment mixture gradually becomes more conservative as their retirement year approaches. In this way, an investor with a retirement target year of 2020 could start with the growth portfolio, shift to the balanced portfolio, and then notch down to either the conservative or income portfolio for the remaining years. Someone who has 12 years to retirement would enter the cycle at the balanced or conservative portfolio level and then shift to the more conservative portfolios as his or her retirement target date approached.

Regardless of where or when you slot into the strategic retirement investment approach, your portfolio should be rebalanced regularly. This ensures that as some investments gain or lose value, your asset allocation will not stray further and further from the selected portfolio profile.

One of the key advantages of a strategic retirement portfolio approach is its flexibility. When you first venture into the workplace, you have no idea whether or not you will build wealth, win the lottery, or retire with a company pension, so it's prudent to select one of the two growth portfolios. As time passes and your life unfolds, you are in a much better position to gauge your future retirement income needs. If you did win the lottery, have made a killing in real estate, or will receive a healthy pension benefit (enough to provide for a secure retirement), then you can afford to keep a higher percent of your investments in stocks.

After starting off with the maximum growth portfolio, you

could, in this scenario, notch down to the growth or balanced port-folio, and remain there until and throughout your retirement. On the other hand, you may find that you're going to have to rely on your strategic retirement portfolio to provide a good part of your retirement income. In that case, as your retirement target year draws closer, you simply keep downshifting to, say, the conservative or income portfolio, as some exposure to stocks will be essential to provide the necessary growth element.

Immunizing Against Downside Risk

Some investors want to remain in a strategic retirement portfolio with a higher percentage of stocks, but can't afford the downside risk to their future retirement income stream. They may want to consider purchasing an insurance wrap to protect their principal. Although there is a cost for this insurance (typically 0.5% to 0.75% a year), it allows investors to increase their chances of starting retire-ment with a higher balance, and at the same time "immunizes" their principal against a bear market. Purchasing this insurance, perhaps seven to 12 years before retirement, would minimize the cost while maximizing the opportunity for further growth.

Final Thoughts

Most investors, whether they admit it or not, are influenced by market movements. A bullish stock market and month after month of positive business headlines can seduce even the most cautious of investors, inclining them towards a more aggressive portfolio. The trouble is, they stay there. It's only when they hit a bear market that they sit up and take notice and resolve to pay more attention to their retirement accounts. Declining balances on their statements tend to have that effect, especially if they are nearing the year they plan to retire. This creates a high level of uncertainty and anxiety. As many people are beginning to realize, simply saving money for retirement is only part of the answer.

The strategic retirement approach gives investors a straightforward investment plan to lock into and stick with. The year when you will retire, in combination with regular rebalancing and systematic shifts to more conservative investments — not the ongoing influence of bull or bear markets — is your key to achieving a secure retirement.

17

Profiting from the
Longevity Revolution

Today we stand on the threshold of a longevity revolution. The aging of the world's population will profoundly alter the structure of the global economy and will have far-reaching social and political implications. Today the elderly — those age 65 and over — in all industrialized countries account for almost 12.5% of the population; by 2025 this proportion is projected to rise to 25%. Moreover, ongoing advances in health care brought about by new drugs and treatments will ensure that this group not only lives longer, but also lives healthily for longer. As a result, the average person in the industrialized nations of the world will now spend one-third of his or her life in retirement, and much of that time will be spent as a "healthy elder."

In addition, the number of people reaching 80 and older — the "old old" — will also grow dramatically. In the United States, while the 65-and-over population will double in the next half century, the 80-and-over population will more than triple. By 2050 there will be over 31 million octogenarians in the United States. In Canada, the octogenarian population is expected to quadruple to just under 4 million by 2050, representing almost 10% of the total population. What's more, it will be the largest segment of Canadian society.

Similar trends can be observed in all the advanced countries. For example, by the year 2050, Japan's octogenarians will account for over 13% of the total population, and in Italy this group will make up

15% of that nation's citizenry. In the United Kingdom, the number of octogenarians is projected to rise to 6 million by the year 2050.

Over the next 50 years, according to the U.S. Census Department, the total population of the major industrialized countries is expected to increase by 96 million, rising from 693 million in 2000 to 788 million in 2050. But what's remarkable about this increase is that it will come almost entirely from unprecedented growth of the 65-and-over age group. During this period, the elderly population is expected to double in the major industrialized countries, rising to close to 200 million by 2050. In sharp contrast, the working-age population — those between 20 and 64 — is expected to decline by 6 million, and the youth population — age 19 years and under — is expected to increase by only 6 million, and actually to decline in Europe and Japan.

A Structural Change

Collectively, the healthy elder and old old groups represent a powerful consumer force, whose participation in the economy will provide businesses with a significant and stable new market. Gone are the days of viewing the elderly as "problems." Today's seniors are healthier and wealthier. Ken Dychtwald, best-selling author of *Age Wave*, noted this in his speech at the Washington, D.C., Center for Strategic and International Studies (CSIS) Policy Summit on Global Aging in January 2000: " . . . people over 50 in the United States now control over $7 trillion of wealth; they represent about 50% of all discretionary spending." What's more, these seniors are going to be consumers for what could be a very long time — 30, 40, or perhaps even 50 more years.

Undoubtedly, this market presents tremendous new opportunities, from robotic limbs to retirement communities to anti-aging drugs and treatments. The fortunes of many companies and industries may well depend on how they adapt to this structural change and rise to the challenge of meeting the needs of this powerful new consumer group.

Growth Opportunities and Industries to Watch

Pharmaceuticals and Genetics

With sales of over $550 billion in 2000, the global pharmaceutical industry, which is dominated by a number of large, multinational enterprises, is growing rapidly. In its 2000 annual report, the Patented Medicine Prices Review Board found that over the past decade, in Canada alone, expenditures on drugs have grown on average at about three times the annual rate of inflation and two times the rate of growth for other components of the health care system. In 2000, Canadians spent $10 billion on drugs for human use, compared to only $3.7 billion in 1990.

Drugs are being brought to the marketplace at an increasingly faster pace. For example, in the United States the time from development to market has been reduced to a low of 10 to 15 years. Given ongoing advances in biotechnology and computer science technology, it won't stop there for long. This, combined with a faster approval process by the U.S. Food and Drug Administration and an increase in patent protection from 17 to 20 years, has ensured a stable future environment for pharmaceutical companies.

Given the new reality of longevity, it should come as no surprise that many of the most highly profitable drugs and personal care products in the marketplace today are those associated with aging. These include Viagra, which accounted for over 90% of all new prescriptions processed in the United States less than a month after it was introduced; Aricept, a memory enhancer; Celebrex, to stop arthritic pain; Fosamax, to help prevent osteoporosis; Rogaine, which promotes hair growth; and Renova, to reduce wrinkles. One can expect this list to grow as companies concentrate their research on the race to be first to market with the next drug or treatment with the potential to enhance longevity. Included here are drugs such as those targeting circulatory disease — the leading cause of death and disability in people over 65 worldwide — and those whose purpose is simply to make us look younger for longer.

In the field of genetic research, as the saying goes, "you ain't seen nothin' yet." In the 1970s, the research cost of deciphering one gene was around US$2.5 million; today, it is about US$100. This tremendous reduction in cost, combined with continuing advances in computer science technology, has permitted scientists to rapidly accelerate their search for the genes that may control lifespan.

Researchers at the California Institute of Technology have reportedly doubled the lifespan of a fruit fly from its typical 37-day duration, and, in a joint study by Canadian and U.S. scientists, a worm's life span was extended from its average of two weeks to two months. These studies of the common fruit fly and the lowly nematode have allowed researchers not only to pinpoint the genes linked to aging, but also to question the inevitability of aging itself. The completion of human DNA sequencing in 2003 by the U.S. Human Genome Project will reveal the biologic map of human life — and set us on a new and exciting stage of evolution, in which the process of human aging could be slowed down or even reversed.

In other areas of genetic research, in 1997 the Scottish firm PPL Therapeutics successfully cloned Dolly the sheep from an adult cell. Early in 2002 the company announced it had cloned pigs that were genetically engineered to help bridge the cross-species barrier. These "knock-out" pigs do not have the gene often rejected by the human body in transplants. This latest advance in genetic engineering brings ever closer the actuality of safely harvesting animal organs for human use, and with it the capability of further lengthening the human lifespan.

Health Care

Because of the structural shift in demand away from people who need short-term care for illness and towards those who will need long-term nursing care, the need for nursing homes and assisted living and long-term care facilities will increase dramatically. As governments alone will be unable to meet this demand, this presents an opportunity for the private sector.

Furthermore, as the number of old old adults increases, so will the number who are relatively fit and wish to maintain health and independence at home. According to the May 1997 issue of *Mobility* magazine, more than half of homeowners age 65 and over lived for 20+ years in their homes, and three out of 10 did so for 30+ years. These "prefer-to-stay-put" seniors will create an additional need for home care nurses, aides, and new service-oriented companies that can provide a total house maintenance package.

Other areas of growth might include companies that provide services and resources for families supporting elderly parents, such as adult daycare facilities and daycare bus services, and companies engaged in the design and manufacture of medical and surgical equipment and implants ranging from bionic limbs, synthetic muscles, and knee and hip replacements, to technology-enhanced vision, hearing, and walking aids.

The Financial Industry

Longer lifespans and the shift away from defined benefit plans, with their guarantee of a specific amount every month for life, mean people will require more help in making suitable financial decisions to ensure that they don't run out of money. The millions of retirees who will have to adjust their thinking — and their investments — to prepare for late-life financial security augurs well for the continued growth of retirement planning and investment management services. More progressive companies will also move to expand their services to include specialized counselling in areas such as the transition from a working life to one of retirement, retirement lifestyles, nursing and retirement homes, and late-life careers.

Insurance companies should also stand to benefit from the increased demand for annuities, investment insurance, and long-term care insurance, as consumers look for protection from uncertain retirement incomes, investment loss, and the possibility of late-life chronic health and mental problems.

Real Estate

The trend in real estate will be away from bedroom communities, with their focus on schools and malls, to homes and retirement residences within an easy commute, or preferably walking distance, of shops, restaurants, medical and continuing education facilities, libraries, and parks. Many retirees and semi-retirees will also favour retirement and waterfront communities, both full ownership and time-share, that offer sports, dining, and social activities.

The Automobile and Travel Industries

Given the declining birth rates, forward-thinking automobile companies are thinking about rolling up their plans for minivans and other family-oriented vehicles. Instead, with an eye to the new growth opportunities presented by seniors, their designers may well be focusing on "smart" cars with elderly-adult-friendly features. These could include such innovations as front seats that swivel 90 degrees for easier entry; night-vision capability; enlarged instrument panels; automated voice alerts for low fuel and oil changes; and easy-access trunks. The recreational vehicle sector of this industry could benefit from catering to seniors who want to travel, but with all the comforts of home.

In the travel industry, the race may be won by airlines and tour bus companies that offer not only superior service and healthy meals, but also super-adjustable seats and leg supports. Hotels, resorts, and cruises will offer customized diet and fitness programs and cosmetic mini-surgery getaways. Packaged theme tours could target hobbies and interests such as gardening, art, shopping, theatre, cooking, wine tasting, birdwatching, and literature.

And there will be others as well. Companies in the technology, food, soft drink, sportswear, cosmetic, clothing, and advertising industries, to name a few, will be lining up to enter the race for the lion's share of the new seniors' market. It will be an interesting competition with, of course, its winners and losers. But far more importantly, the end result should provide an abundance of choice, not only for the healthy elders, but also for the old old.

The following questions are designed to help employees find out more about their company pension plan. To get the answers to these queries, ask your employer's plan manager or whoever is responsible within your company, typically someone in the human resources department. For general information on the different types of employer-sponsored plans such as defined benefit (DB), defined contribution (DC), group registered retirement savings plans (group RRSPs), and deferred profit-sharing plans (DPSPs), see Chapter 9.

	Yes	No
Does your company have a pension plan?	___	___
Are you included in, or can you join, the plan?	___	___
Do you know what type of plan (DB, DC, group RRSP, or DPSP) it is?	___	___
If it is a defined benefit plan, do you know the formula used?	___	___
Have you worked long enough to be vested?	___	___
Will you receive a regular statement of contributions?	___	___
Is there a cap on the number of years for which you can earn benefits?	___	___
Does the company plan have different investment options?	___	___

	Yes	No
Have you obtained a projection of your likely income at retirement?	____	____
Will your pension be integrated with the Canada or Quebec Pension Plan (C/QPP)?	____	____
Is the pension fully or partially indexed to inflation?	____	____
Can you transfer your pension to a registered retirement income fund (RRIF)?*	____	____
Can you transfer your pension to a life income fund (LIF) or locked-in retirement income fund (LRIF)?**	____	____
If you can transfer, are there any age restrictions?	____	____
Do you know what will happen to your pension if you retire early?	____	____
Do you know what will happen to your pension if you change jobs?	____	____
Do you know what will happen to your pension when you die?	____	____
Is your pension insured?	____	____

* For more on RRIFs, see Chapter 11.
** For more on LIFs and LRIFs, see Chapter 12.

Retirement Expenses Worksheet

A Prelude to the Retirement Expenses Worksheet

Before you begin filling out the Retirement Expenses Worksheet, it's important to keep in mind some pertinent realities:

- *Canadians are living longer.* On average, men can expect to live until 82 years of age, and women until 85. To enjoy those extra years you'll probably need to accumulate additional savings to make sure your standard of living does not deteriorate as the decades pass.
- *Canadians are staying healthier for longer.* As a healthy, younger-feeling and -looking retiree, your lifestyle might include many more years of active sports and leisure activities than those of your parents' generation. You want to make certain that you have budgeted enough extra money to cover the costs of funding these pastimes.
- *Some expenses may decrease.* When you retire, your annual income will probably be less, so your taxes will be lower. You'll also no longer be paying for employment insurance, contributing to a pension plan, or have any other job-related expenses. What's more, by age 65 your house may be paid for, you may be contemplating moving to less expensive accommodation, and your children's education costs have generally been taken care of.
- *Some expenses may linger.* Your mortgage may not be paid off by the time you quit working, so you may have to factor this expense

into your budget for the initial phase of your retirement. Although most life insurance policies are paid up by age 65, some require premiums until 71 years of age. Depending on their age of retirement and other factors, some parents may still have children or others that require financial support.

- *Some expenses may increase.* Depending on your ongoing physical condition and whether your previous employer continues to provide health insurance coverage, supplemental medical, dental, and other health care costs could rise significantly. You may also decide to purchase long-term care insurance to guard against the costs of extended stays in nursing homes. With more leisure time, recreation and entertainment expenses could increase substantially. Also, the general costs of living, such as food, running a car, clothing, and personal care expenses, will in all likelihood rise over time.

Retirement Lifestyles

You should spend some time visualizing the type of retirement lifestyle you want. This will give you a better idea of not only where your money will be spent, but also how much you are going to need. Depending on the type of retirement you envisage, you may have to do a little background research to determine some of the associated costs.

For instance, if your retirement dream is to buy a boat and live on it anchored off an island in the Strait of Georgia, you'll need to establish how you are going to accomplish this and what the accompanying price tag is. You might intend to do a straight switch by selling your home and buying the boat. Or you may need a loan to cover all or some of the costs. In addition, you would need to factor in the annual costs of boat ownership. On the other hand, you might simply want to stay put, with no drastic changes to your lifestyle. But even then, with many additional hours of leisure time, you may want to consider allocating some extra money for hobbies.

Retirement Expenses Worksheet

You can estimate your retirement expenses on either a monthly or yearly basis, whichever you prefer. If you select a monthly estimate, simply multiply by 12 to arrive at the annual amount. Keep in mind that because the Retirement Income Gap Worksheet in Appendix C, Table 1, takes into account a 3% inflation rate, there is no need to factor inflation into your calculations.

As a rough rule of thumb, you can typically expect retirement expenses to be around 65% to 70% of your current income. Of course, depending on the type of lifestyle you want to lead when you retire, your expenses could be much more or substantially less.

Retirement Expenses Worksheet

	Estimated $ Amount at Retirement	
Expenses	**Monthly**	**Annually**
1. Housing	_____	_____
(mortgage payments, rent, insurance, taxes, utilities, and maintenance costs such as putting on a new roof or repaving the driveway)		
2. Transportation	_____	_____
(gas, insurance, maintenance, public transportation)		
3. Insurance	_____	_____
(life, medical and dental, long-term care)		
4. Income tax	_____	_____
5. Clothing and personal care	_____	_____
6. Dependent children or other family members	_____	_____

7. *Travel and entertainment*
   (hobbies, sports, vacations, restaurants)

8. *Miscellaneous purchases*
   (home furnishings, replacing appliances)

9. *Loan Payments*
   (If appropriate, large-ticket items such as
   a car, recreational vehicle, or boat could
   be included here.)

10. **Total estimated annual**
    retirement expenses

Appendix C
Retirement Income
Gap Worksheet

Filling out this worksheet is a crucial step towards making certain that you reach your retirement goals. The outcome will tell you whether you are on track to meeting your aspirations. If you are not, it will identify your projected income gap. It will also show you how much you need to save each year to fill that gap and reach your desired retirement goal.

Follow the example as a guide to completing the worksheet. The example assumes retirement in 30 years, sources of income at retirement of $20,000, and an annual income goal of $50,000 over a 30-year retirement. The income of $20,000 includes the maximum benefit of around $5,000 from Old Age Security, an annual $7,000 benefit from the Canada Pension Plan, and $8,000 from a defined benefit pension plan. The example also takes into account current RRSP savings of $50,000 and annual contributions of $2,000 until retirement.

To determine how much you will get from Old Age Security, see Chapter 8, and for the Canada/Quebec Pension Plan, refer to your Statement of Contributions. Or, if you prefer, you can call the telephone numbers listed in Fast Facts about Canada's Public Pension System in Appendix D. When it comes to company pension plans, if you contribute to a defined benefit or deferred profit-sharing plan, contact your employer's plan manager for the future value of either of these pensions. If you contribute to a defined contribution plan or group RRSP, use Table C2 to estimate the future value of savings in these company plans. If a higher percentage of your savings is invested in equities, you can assume a higher rate of return. On the other hand, lower returns should be assumed with a mostly fixed-income portfolio.

Another potential source of retirement income is, of course, your home. Many retirees downsize (move to less expensive accommodation) and use the remaining proceeds to provide a flow of income. If you are planning to take this route, you can include the dollar amount you expect to realize on line 8 in the Worksheet. For instance, if you anticipate selling your home for $300,000, after deducting about $20,000 for legal, realtor, and other costs, you would be left with $280,000. From this amount, if appropriate, you would also have to deduct any outstanding mortgage balance and the cost of purchasing a new home.

If you do plan to sell your home at retirement, there are two key points you should bear in mind. The first is that, as real estate is fairly illiquid, it may take you much longer to sell your home than you anticipate. And second, it's best to be conservative when estimating its future value. In other words, plan on your home's being on the market for a longer, instead of a shorter period, and also on getting less for it, rather than more. This cautious approach will act as a safeguard against dealing with unexpected income shortfall at retirement. Of course, if you are planning to remain in your family home when you retire, simply leave line 8 blank.

Retirement Income Gap Worksheet

	Yours	Example
1. Annual retirement income goal (from Appendix B, line 10)	$ _____	$ 50,000
2. Sources of Income		
a) Old Age Security	$ _____	$ 5,000
b) Canada/Quebec Pension Plan	$ _____	$ 7,000
c) company pension	$ _____	$ 8,000
d) other income (rental property, employment income)	$ _____	$ 0

3. Total income
   (Add lines 2a through 2d) $ _____ $ 20,000

4. Retirement income gap
   (line 1 minus line 3) $ _____ $ 30,000

5. Total savings needed at retirement $ _____ $ 903,600
   (Table C1, 30-year column, line 7)

6. Savings already accumulated for
   retirement (RRSPs, other savings) $ _____ $ 50,000

7. Value of current savings at retirement $ _____ $ 380,500
   (Table C2, 7% column, line 6:
   $ 50,000 x 7.61)

8. Anticipated value of home $ _____ $ 0

9. Savings shortfall at retirement
   (line 5 minus total of lines 7 and 8) $ _____ $ 523,100

10. Annual savings needed to reach $ _____ $ 5,545
    retirement income goal
    (Table C3, 30-year column:
    $ 500,000 = $ 5,300;
    $ 10,000 x 2 = $ 212;
    $ 1,000 x 3 = $ 33)

11. Current annual savings $ _____ $ 2,000

12. Additional annual savings needed to
    reach retirement income goal
    (line 10 minus line 11) $ _____ $ 3,545

Table C1

Total Savings Needed at Retirement

If your retirement income gap is:				Years to Retirement				
	5	10	15	20	25	30	35	40
$ 1,000	$ 14,385	$ 16,677	$ 19,333	$ 22,412	$ 25,982	$ 30,120	$ 34,917	$ 40,479
5,000	71,927	83,383	96,664	112,060	129,908	150,600	174,586	202,393
10,000	143,854	166,766	193,328	224,120	259,816	301,200	349,172	404,786
15,000	215,781	250,149	289,992	336,180	389,724	451,800	523,758	607,179
20,000	287,708	333,532	386,656	448,240	519,632	602,400	698,344	809,572
25,000	359,635	416,915	483,320	560,300	649,540	753,000	872,930	1,011,965
30,000	431,562	500,298	579,984	672,360	779,448	903,600	1,047,516	1,214,358
40,000	575,416	667,064	773,312	896,480	1,039,264	1,204,800	1,396,688	1,619,144
50,000	719,270	833,830	966,640	1,120,600	1,299,080	1,506,000	1,745,860	2,023,930

(assumes 7% compound annual return and annual inflation of 3%)

How to Use Table C1: Total Savings Needed at Retirement

Let's say that on Line 4 of the Retirement Income Gap Worksheet you have determined that you have a retirement income gap of $20,000 and you have 15 years to go before you retire. Find the $20,000 figure in Column 1 of Table C1 and, on the same line, the dollar amount under the appropriate number of years to retirement, in this case 15. This shows that you have to save an additional $386,656 in the remaining 15 years before you retire. This is the amount that you would enter on Line 5 of your worksheet: Total savings needed at retirement.

If, on the other hand, you are retiring in 35 years, but with the same $20,000 retirement income gap, you would require $698,344 — substantially more. This increase in the total amount required is entirely due to the effects of inflation on the value of a dollar. In other words, your dollar is worth less over time, so you have to save more in order to compensate. In this table we have assumed a 3% rate of inflation, the historical average for Canada.

For a retirement income gap that is an odd amount, such as $13,000 or $28,000, you might want to grab a calculator. A retirement in, say, 10 years, with a gap of $13,000, requires two steps. First, locate the $10,000 figure in Column 1 and, on the same line, the dollar amount under 10 years to retirement, which will give you $166,766. Next, go to the $1,000 line and find the dollar amount; multiply by three (in our example, $16,677 x 3 = $50,031). So in order to close your retirement income gap of $13,000 in 10 years, additional savings of $216,797 ($166,766 + $50,031) would be required.

How to Use Table C2: Factor to Determine Future Value of Savings

This is a useful table for calculating what your current savings are going to be worth at some future date. The only component you have to determine is your expected rate of return. Here it's best to err on

Table C2

Factors to Determine Future Value of Savings

Years to Retirement	Rate of Return					
	5%	6%	7%	8%	9%	10%
5	1.28	1.34	1.40	1.47	1.54	1.61
10	1.63	1.79	1.97	2.16	2.37	2.59
15	2.08	2.40	2.76	3.17	3.64	4.18
20	2.65	3.21	3.87	4.66	5.60	6.73
25	3.39	4.29	5.43	6.85	8.62	10.83
30	4.32	5.74	7.61	10.06	13.27	17.45
35	5.52	7.69	10.68	14.79	20.41	28.10
40	7.04	10.29	14.97	21.72	31.41	45.26

the side of caution and assume a lower return rather than a higher return. That way, you lessen the chances of having an income shortfall at retirement.

To use the table, simply determine the number of years until you retire, select an appropriate rate of return, and multiply your current savings by the factor indicated. For instance, assuming a 10% rate of return, $100,000 in current savings will grow in 10 years to $259,000 ($100,000 x 2.59). Assuming a 6% rate of return, the same $100,000 will provide only $179,000 ($100,000 x 1.79). At retirement, if you had assumed the higher rate of return and your investments actually delivered only 6%, you would be faced with an asset shortfall of $80,000.

How to Use Table C3: Annual Savings Needed to Reach Retirement Income Goal

The first fact that will strike you about this table is that the closer you are to your retirement, the more you will have to save annually in order to meet your income goal. For instance, let's take the case of someone wishing to retire at age 65 with a nest egg of half a million dollars. At age 60, he would need savings of $86,940 a year to

Table C3

Annual Savings Needed to Reach Retirement Income Goal

If your savings shortfall is:				Years to Retirement				
	5	10	15	20	25	30	35	40
$ 1,000	$ 174	$ 75	$ 40	$ 24	$ 16	$ 11	$ 7	$ 5
10,000	1,739	724	398	244	158	106	72	50
25,000	4,347	1,809	995	610	395	265	181	125
50,000	8,694	3,618	1,990	1,220	790	530	362	250
75,000	13,041	5,427	2,985	1,830	1,185	795	543	375
100,000	17,388	7,236	3,980	2,440	1,580	1,060	724	500
150,000	26,082	10,854	5,970	3,660	2,370	1,590	1,086	750
200,000	34,776	14,472	7,960	4,880	3,160	2,120	1,448	1,000
250,000	43,470	18,090	9,950	6,100	3,950	2,650	1,810	1,250
300,000	52,164	21,708	11,940	7,320	4,740	3,180	2,172	1,500
400,000	69,552	28,944	15,920	9,760	6,320	4,240	2,896	2,000
500,000	86,940	36,180	19,900	12,200	7,900	5,300	3,620	2,500

(assumes 7% compound annual return)

reach the required goal. This level of savings would be out of reach for most of us. In sharp contrast, at age 25, with 40 years until retirement, savings of only $2,500 a year would easily attain that $500,000 nest egg — certainly within the grasp of many Canadians.

To use Table C3, you need the dollar amount arrived at on line 9 (savings shortfall at retirement) in the Retirement Income Gap Worksheet on page 161. Locate the appropriate savings shortfall in the left-hand column of Table C3 and find to the right the relevant number of years to retirement. The dollar amount indicated is the amount you need to save every year to reach your retirement income goal. For instance, let's assume your savings shortfall is $100,000 and you have 20 years until retirement. In this instance, you would have to save $2,440 a year for the next 20 years to meet your retirement income goal (line 6, column 5). However, if you have only 10 years to go, you would have to save considerably more per year: $7,236 (line 6, column 3).

For odd amounts, as with Table C1, you may want to use a calculator. For illustration purposes, let's say you have a savings shortfall of $17,000 and 15 years to go before you retire. First, locate $10,000 in column 1 of Table C3 and, on the same line, the dollar amount under 15 years to retirement, which will give you an amount of $398. Next, go to the $1,000 line, find the dollar amount, and multiply by seven. In this case, $40 x 7 = $280. So in order to make up the savings shortfall of $17,000 and reach your retirement income goal, an annual savings of $678 ($398 + $280) would be required over the next 15 years.

Fast Facts about
Canada's Public Pension System

You can contact the telephone numbers in this appendix to get information about the Canada/Quebec Pension Plan (C/QPP) or Old Age Security (OAS). For specific information on *your* benefits, you will need the number that appears on your C/QPP or OAS payment, your Social Insurance Number (SIN), or the number on your OAS card. As lines are busiest at the beginning and end of each month, it's best to call at other times.

For information on the Canada Pension Plan or Old Age Security, contact Human Resources Development Canada (HRDC) at

1-800-277-9914 (English)
1-800-277-9915 (French)
1-800-255-4786 (TDD/TTY)

Or, if you have Internet access, visit their Web site at <www.hrdc-drhc.gc.ca/isp>.

For information on the Quebec Pension Plan, check your Quebec telephone directory for the nearest office of the Régie des rentes du Quebec.

Key Points about the Canada/Quebec Pension Plan (C/QPP)

- The C/QPP covers working Canadians between 18 and 70 years of age with annual earned incomes of between $3,500 and the average wage ($38,300 for 2001).
- It pays retirement pensions, survivor benefits, children's benefits, disability benefits, and a lump-sum death benefit.
- All benefits must be applied for; they are not sent automatically. It is recommended that you apply at least six months before you want to start receiving benefits. For an application form, call 1-877-454-4051.
- Retirement pensions can be applied for as early as age 60 with a 0.5% reduction for each month you are under 65 (which is considered the normal retirement age), up to a maximum reduction of 30%. If you start receiving your pension after age 65, your benefit will be increased by 0.5% for every month you are over the normal retirement age, again, up to a maximum of 30%.
- The maximum monthly pension rates for 2001 were $542.50 at age 60, $775 at age 65, and $1,007.50 at 70 years of age. The average monthly benefit at age 65 was $417.23.
- Spouses or common-law partners (of either sex) who meet certain requirements can elect to pension-split. This sharing of pensions could help reduce taxes by moving the higher income earner into a lower tax bracket. For more information on sharing benefits or to obtain copies of the appropriate forms, call 1-877-454-4051.
- All benefits are considered taxable income.
- Pension benefits can be paid to you anywhere in the world.

Key Points about Old Age Security (OAS)

- The basic monthly pension ($110.66 for 2001) is payable to all eligible Canadians age 65 years or over who have lived in Canada for at least 10 years after reaching age 18.
- The maximum monthly benefit for 2001 was $442.66.

- OAS benefits must be applied for; they are not sent automatically. It is recommended that you apply for this benefit about six months before you reach 65. For an application form, call 1-877-454-4051.
- You do not have to be retired to receive this pension.
- OAS pensions are taxable income.
- Provided you have resided in Canada for a least 20 years after age 18, you can live outside Canada and receive benefits no matter which country you choose to reside in.

The Guaranteed Income Supplement and Allowance

The GIS and Allowance provide additional income to low-income seniors living in Canada. To qualify for either of these tax-free benefits, your yearly income must fall below certain limits. To find out more about these benefits, see Chapter 9, or call 1-800-277-9914.

Glossary

allowance: formerly Spouse's Pension Allowance, a non-taxable monthly benefit paid to low-income individuals age 60 to 64 who are the spouses or widow(er)s of Old Age Security pensioners.

annuity: a regular pension or similar benefit that is paid out for a contracted number of years, or for the lifetime of the beneficiary, from an invested lump sum of capital.

bank rate: the minimum lending rate of the Bank of Canada. Changes in the bank rate often lead to changes in the prime rate, which is the rate of interest that commercial banks charge to their lowest-risk customers. Other rates can be affected, including those for mortgages, cars, and business loans, as well as rates paid to savers on deposits and investment certificates.

beneficiary: the designated recipient of assets, such as the proceeds of an insurance policy, trust, or registered plan.

bond: a type of long-term debt instrument that promises to pay the holder a specified amount of interest and to return the principal amount on a specified maturity date.

Canada Customs and Revenue Agency (CCRA): formerly Revenue Canada. This federal government organization issues regulations regarding registered plans in Canada.

Canada Pension Plan (CPP): a contributory, earnings-related social insurance program that ensures a measure of income protection to contributors and their families against the loss of income due to retirement, disability, or death. The plan operates throughout Canada, except in the province of Quebec, where a similar program, the Quebec Pension Plan (QPP), is in effect.

Canada Savings Bonds (CSBs): bonds issued each year by the federal government that pay a competitive rate of interest that is guaranteed for one or more years. They may be cashed in at any time; after the first three months, CSBs pay interest up to the end of the month prior to encashment.

capital gain: An increase in the monetary value of a capital asset such as a share, bond, property, or other asset, which results in a profit if the asset is sold. If a share is bought at $26 and sold at $30, there is a capital gain of $4.

Consumer Price Index (CPI): a measure of price changes produced by Statistics Canada on a monthly basis. The CPI measures the retail prices of a "shopping basket" of about 300 goods and services, including food, housing, transportation, clothing, and recreation. The index is weighted, meaning that it gives greater importance to price changes for some products than for others — more to housing, for example, than to entertainment — in an effort to reflect typical spending patterns. The CPI is also referred to as the cost of living.

debt: an obligation to pay an amount due (and interest, if required) under specified terms.

deferred profit-sharing plan (DPSP): a plan registered under the Income Tax Act into which an employer may make tax-deductible contributions based on the profits of the company, on behalf of its employees. Payments received by employees from the plan are taxable.

defined benefit (DB) pension plan: a plan that provides a pension that is generally based on final average or best average earnings and years of service. Under the Income Tax Act, the amount of defined benefit pension that can be provided under a registered plan is limited, in general terms, to the lesser of 2% of the employee's best average earnings or $1,722 per year of service. Starting in 2005, the $1,722 limit will be indexed to increases in the average wage.

defined contribution (DC) pension plan: a plan, also known as a money purchase plan, that provides a pension. With this type of plan you are not promised a set benefit or pension at retirement. Rather, an individual account is opened in your name, and your final benefits depend on how much is contributed and the rate of return earned by the accounts investments.

diversification: investment in a number of unrelated or partially interdependent financial assets to reduce risk and achieve a more stable portfolio.

dividend: a portion of a company's profit that is distributed to shareholders in proportion to the number of shares they hold.

earned income: for tax purposes, generally the money made by an individual from employment and some taxable benefits. Earned income is used as the basis for calculating RRSP maximum contribution limits.

financial planning: the process of assessing your financial situation, determining your objectives, and formulating a plan to achieve them.

Group of Seven (G7): the world's seven largest industrial market economies: the United States, Japan, Germany, France, Britain, Italy, and Canada. The leaders of these countries meet annually to discuss political and economic issues of mutual concern.

Guaranteed Income Supplement (GIS): a non-taxable monthly benefit paid to lower-income Old Age Security recipients on the basis of family income. Benefits are fully phased out at specific net income levels for both individuals and couples.

income: a combination of wages, interest, dividends, realized capital gains, private and public pension payments, rents, royalties, net business income, and self-employment income.

inflation: the average rate of increase in prices, usually measured as a percentage increase in the consumer price index (CPI). Canada's inflation target, as set out by the federal government and the Bank of Canada, aims to keep it within a range of 1% to 3%.

interest: payments made by a borrower to a lender for the use of his or her money. Interest is paid on deposits because they are, in effect, loans to a bank or other deposit-taking institution.

interest rate: interest payable on a debt expressed as a percentage of the debt over a period of time (usually a year). If a loan's interest rate is 10% annually, you pay $10 interest each year for every $100 borrowed.

investment income: income received from investments, such as bonds and stocks, and from rental property.

labour force: a country's number of people 15 years of age or over who either have a job or are actively looking for one.

labour productivity: a measure of how much output an economy produces per worker, that is, the gross domestic product (GDP) per worker.

life income fund (LIF): a mechanism for converting a matured locked-in registered retirement savings plan or retirement account.

Withdrawals from a LIF are similar to those from a registered retirement income fund (RRIF), but provincial pension benefit acts and the federal Pension Benefits Standards Act impose limits on the maximum amount that can be withdrawn annually from a LIF.

locked-in retirement account (LIRA): sometimes called a locked-in RRSP, an account that contains accumulated pension benefits transferred out of a workplace pension plan.

locked-in registered retirement savings plan (RRSP): a plan set up to receive funds transferred from a registered company pension plan, on the condition that it be used solely for retirement income purposes.

long-term interest rate: an interest rate applying to money lent for a period of 10 years or more. Typically, long-term rates are higher than short-term rates because lenders demand a higher return for tying up their money for a lengthy period.

means testing: a formula used when the level of a benefit is based on the recipient's income level. As net income rises, means-tested benefits such as Old Age Security decrease.

money market instruments: a range of interest-bearing short-term investments with maturities of less than one year.

mutual fund: a fund operated by a professional investment firm that raises money from shareholders and invests it in a variety of investments, such as stocks, bonds, money market instruments, futures, and commodities.

net income: for tax purposes, total income minus allowable deductions such as pension contributions, union dues, and child care expenses. A single individual with total income of $52,000 and a registered retirement savings plan deduction of $5,000 would report his or her net income for personal income tax purposes as $47,000.

non-registered investments: non–tax-sheltered investments, or those on which earnings are recognized as income in the year they are earned and taxed according to Canada Customs and Revenue Agency regulations.

Old Age Security (OAS): a universal federal benefit provided to retired Canadians age 65 and older. OAS benefits are taxable and are reduced for individuals with net income in excess of $55,309.

personal income: income received by an individual from all possible sources.

personal income tax: tax on personal income, including both federal and provincial personal income taxes.

Quebec Pension Plan (QPP): a contributory, earnings-related social insurance program that ensures a measure of income protection to contributors and their families against the loss of income due to retirement, disability, or death. The plan operates only in Quebec; throughout the rest of Canada, a similar program, the Canada Pension Plan (CPP), is in effect.

real interest rate: the nominal interest rate minus the inflation rate. All else being equal, the higher the current inflation rate, the higher the nominal interest rates will be. With a nominal interest rate of 10% on a loan and inflation at 3%, the real interest rate is 7% (10% – 3%).

rate of return: the level of earnings attained or expected from an investment over a period of time.

real rate of return: the rate of return adjusted to take inflation into account.

registered investment: an investment recognized by the Canada Customs and Revenue Agency that allows individuals to defer paying income tax on principal and earnings until the income is withdrawn from the account.

registered pension plan (RPP): a pension plan for employees sponsored by employers or unions and usually funded by contributions by both employees and employers. Contributions to RPPs are tax-deductible, the investment income in them is tax-deferred, and withdrawals from them are taxable.

registered retirement income fund (RRIF): a fund for individuals that provides income in retirement. RRIFs are set up by directly transferring monies from registered retirement savings plans or from lump-sum payments from registered pension plans. A minimum amount must be withdrawn from a RRIF each year, beginning in the year after the RRIF is established. All withdrawals from RRIFs are taxable.

registered retirement savings plan (RRSP): a savings plan for individuals, including the self-employed. These plans provide income at retirement based on accumulated contributions and return on investment in the plan. Contributions to an RRSP are tax-deductible, the investment income in it is tax-deferred, and payments from it are taxable.

savings rate: personal savings expressed as a percentage of disposable income, which is the income remaining after income taxes and payroll taxes are accounted for.

social assistance: payments made to Canadians on the basis of need by provinces and municipalities, aided by federal contributions under the Canada Health and Social Transfer.

social security: society's commitment to take care of its most vulnerable citizens, such as people without work, single parents with limited means, children in poverty, and people who face barriers to employment due to disability or chronic illness. The "social safety net" comprises a wide range of federal, provincial, and joint federal-provincial programs such as Old Age Security, the Guaranteed Income Supplement, the Canada and Quebec Pension Plans, and employment insurance.

structural change: a fundamental and permanent change in the way an economy generates employment and wealth.

survivor benefits: benefits to which a surviving spouse or other specified beneficiary is entitled upon the death of the policy- or plan-holder. The source of the benefits may be life insurance, a will, or registered account proceeds.

taxable income: net income minus certain allowable deductions. In most cases, a tax filer's taxable income will be the same as his or her net income.

withholding tax: an amount of money that a financial institution is legally obliged to withhold at source and remit to Canada Customs and Revenue Agency on funds withdrawn from an RRSP or on RRIF income payments that exceed the minimum annual income payment amount.

About the Authors

Ranga Chand is recognized as one of Canada's leading economists and mutual fund analysts. He has held senior positions with the federal Department of Finance, later serving as a director of the Conference Board of Canada before joining a major stock brokerage. He has also taught economics at the University of Waterloo, published extensively in the field of economics, and represented Canada at numerous economic forums, including the OECD in Paris, the United Nations, and the World Institute of Economics in Germany. Ranga can be seen every Monday at 3:00 p.m. and 8:30 p.m. EST on ROBTV's popular show *Talking Mutual Funds with Ranga Chand*. He is the author of the annual guide *Chand's Top 50 Mutual Funds* and the annual U.S. guide *Best of the Best Mutual Funds*, featuring America's top 50 Heavy Hitter funds, and co-author of *Ranga Chand's Getting Started with Mutual Funds*.

Sylvia Carmichael is a managing partner with Chand Carmichael & Company Limited. A researcher and writer, she is a business college graduate who has worked with the International Monetary Fund in Washington, D.C., and with the British High Commission in Ottawa. She is also the co-author of *Ranga Chand's Getting Started with Mutual Funds*.